"Not preoccupied with special gifts or manifestations, [Gesswein tells] with biblical precision how every believer can receive ~~~~th the Holy Spirit."

E. Coleman,
—ld Mission
an⸺ ⸺ University

"For the se⸺, this book will open the door to the most exciting life imaginable! It will refreshingly reinforce those who are already experiencing the life controlled by the Holy Spirit."

—*Dr. Bill Bright,*
Founder and President
Campus Crusade for Christ International

"Armin Gesswein knows more about spiritual revival and has taken part in more revivals than any living person. For depth, for balance, for insight, [this book] promises to be an enduring classic."

—*Dr. Sherwood E. Wirt,*
Editor Emeritus, *Decision magazine*

"It is a welcome change to have a book that contributes to unity and clarity on this vital doctrine. . . . *How Can I Be Filled with the Holy Spirit?* has two main distinguishing features. The first is the freshness of Dr. Gesswein's approach to the Word of God. . . . Secondly, I appreciate the faithfulness of his adherence to the Word of God. . . . The author majors on what the Scriptures have to say. His treatment of the Apostle John's writings is particularly enlightening and enriching. Every pastor and lay leader should read this book with prayerful discernment. It will bless them and their ministry."

—*Dr. Stephen Olford,*
Founder, Stephen Olford Center
for Biblical Preaching

"Armin Gesswein is one of the most refreshing Christians I have ever met. . . . He writes like he speaks—with unique voice—to the point, with minimal illustrations and unflourished language. It adds up to a fresh word on an irreplaceable biblical truth that has often suffered from abuse."

—*Dr. David L. Rambo,*
President, Alliance Theological Seminary

How Can I Be Filled with the Holy Spirit?

Biblical Truth and Personal Testimony

Armin R. Gesswein

CHRISTIAN PUBLICATIONS, INC.
CAMP HILL, PENNSYLVANIA

Christian Publications, Inc.
3825 Hartzdale Drive, Camp Hill, PA 17011
www.cpi-horizon.com

Faithful, biblical publishing since 1883

ISBN: 0-87509-813-4

99 00 01 02 03   5 4 3 2 1

Unless otherwise indicated,
all Scripture taken from the
New King James Version of the Bible,
© 1982, 1994 by Thomas Nelson, Inc.

Scripture labeled "KJV" is taken
from the King James Version of the Bible.

to Reidun

**My lifetime sweetheart
and unfailing helper**

Contents

Part 1
Filled with the Spirit:
A Fresh Approach

Chapter 1

Why John?

Chapter 2

*John 17 . . . A New Kind of Unity . . .
Christ Manifests the Glory of God . . . A
Bi-level Gospel . . . Never Change Your
Center . . . We Must Keep the Unity of the
Spirit . . . Jesus Never Sectarianizes . . .
John Fits Between Luke and Acts*

Paul Also Uses the Original Language . . .
Peter, Paul and John in Agreement . . .
Paul in Ephesians

Chapter 6

Receive the Holy Spirit . . . Same Word
"Receive" for Two Distinct Experiences . . .
Let's Not Sectarianize the Holy Spirit . . .
Spirit-filled Life Is Normal . . . Is the
Holy Spirit Given for Sanctification or
for Service? . . . John Clarifies Every-
thing . . . Final Thoughts on John 20:19-
23 . . . The Larger Picture

Part 3
Testimonies

Chapter 7

Chapter 8

Preface

Early in my life, I spent seven months seeking to be filled with the Holy Spirit. I searched Scripture, and I soon found that there is what we can call a twofold Christian life: *born* of the Spirit and *filled* with the Spirit.

This quickly turned into a double search: *I* searched even the Greek roots of the New Testament, and *God* was also searching me, through and through, to my roots. And they were not Greek; they went all the way back to Adam.

My search took me to many kinds of meetings and altars of prayer—sometimes all night, and sometimes half-nights.

During those months God taught me many

things. He also alerted me to many dangers, especially the danger of seeking manifestations of the Holy Spirit.

Did God answer my prayer to be filled? Yes, He did—wonderfully—just perfect for me. He also gave me certain manifestations—gifts—sovereignly ("as He wills") suited for my life and purpose and ministry (1 Corinthians 12).

You too may be having certain struggles concerning the work of the Holy Spirit, so I'll share some of my own with the prayer that you may find help and clarity in your search.

I'm eager to share a fresh discovery which greatly clarifies and simplifies the "how to enter in" experience.

The exciting thing is that it is found in such plain Scripture. The wonder is not only that we could miss seeing it, but that we would take so long.

Introduction

$\mathcal{I}$have experienced a lot of revival, giving messages on how to be filled with the Holy Spirit. And the Lord seemed to use my personal testimony in a special way.

Today new things are happening, and many are entering into widely varied experiences. At the same time many others are confused about what is happening—especially troublesome are some of the demonstrations and manifestations which are taking place.

What seems to be the way to be filled for some is a stumbling block for others. This does not happen in Scripture, and it should not happen with us in the Church. Scripture makes clear that the Spirit-filled Christian life is God's will and promise and command for every Christian and for every church.

I've often said, "The future is with the charismatics." (By "charismatics" I don't mean every-thing going on under that name.) We are in a new day (as Jesus called it) since Pentecost. The *real* "new age" began on that day. Jesus told all about it in John 14-16.

Listen to These Leaders

A young Christian leader said to me that he needed to get the Holy Spirit in focus. "I al-ways knew He was 'there,'" he said, "but I need clarity and focus."

That's pretty much what this book is all about.

On TV I was surprised to hear Rev. David Y. Cho (pastor of the world-famous Yoida Church in Seoul, Korea) say that he wanted to know the Holy Spirit more as a *person*, and not so much as a series of charismatic gifts and their manifestations. Rev. Cho was right on target with Scripture.

In the days of my early ministry on Long Is-land I heard that Dr. Jonathan Goforth was to speak to the students of Nyack Training Insti-tute, New York. His book *By My Spirit*, the story of strong revivals under his ministry in China, had been a great blessing to me. God had visited my church with revival (my first), and there He also called me to a ministry of revival.

2

So another young preacher and I went to Nyack to hear Dr. Goforth. We arrived early, so we boldly went to find his room. His wife opened the door. She was very glad to see us, for she wanted to find someone to lead her husband (now blind and about seventy years of age) across the compound to the chapel where he was to speak.

What a memorable walk! Each of us held an arm as we led him to the chapel. *Here's my chance to ask him a question,* I thought. So as we were walking past the enclosure where Dr. A.B. Simpson is buried, I said, "Dr. Goforth, what is the greatest need in the Church today?" Patting my hand with his, as we were about to enter the door of the chapel, he replied: "The Holy Spirit—the Church hardly knows the Holy Spirit."

A few years later, in the summer of 1938, another friend and I went to hear Dr. G. Campbell Morgan in the Westminster Chapel, London. It was a Friday night, and the chapel was very full. We had recently been in Norway where God was at work in revival power. At the close of the service I said to my friend, "Let's try to meet Dr. Morgan." People had lined up to greet him in his study in the rear of the chapel. "I'm going to have a question ready for him," I told my friend. Dr. Morgan was then eighty, looking very alert sitting behind his desk.

"Dr. Morgan," I asked, "what do you think is the greatest need in the Church today?" At once he replied: "The Holy Spirit—the Church hardly knows the Holy Spirit. . . . I don't mean 'second blessing,' but the *Holy Spirit.*"

These words by two famous, godly men still ring in my ears.

Writing in his book *The Full Blessing of Pentecost*, Andrew Murray says much the same thing: "The Church of today is suffering for the lack of one thing only, the heavenly enduement of power which made the apostolic Church triumphant—the Pentecostal Spirit."

I also like what Andrew Jukes wrote:

> We don't expect half enough from Him [the Holy Spirit]. If the evil spirit is so ready to return to what he calls "his house," with seven other spirits more wicked than himself, what will the Holy Spirit do, if only we can wait for "the promise of the Father"? Will He not come with all His sevenfold power to turn carnal disciples, who have known Christ in

the flesh, to do His works and minister the Spirit as they have never done before? Shall the evil, selfish, hellish spirit do more for his slaves than the Spirit of God does for His own children?[1]

My ministry goes as far as the Church is found, and also as far as the curse is found. I would love to refer to the writings of more great people of God, but we must get right into what *God* has to say in His Word.

Back to the Drawing Board

When I sought to be filled, I was amazed to see how many splits there were among those who professed to be Spirit-filled—just where one would expect to find anything but that. I had expected everyone would be of one heart and mind, "lov[ing] one another fervently with a pure heart" (1 Peter 1:22). The contrast between my ideals and reality confused me greatly, and I could have allowed it to make me stumble and give it all up.

The whole "charismatic" field has become a minefield, and many people avoid it altogether. Questions arise: How can we tell the difference between wildfire and the real fire of the Holy Spirit? How can we keep from throwing the baby out with the bathwater in this matter? What is the difference between a soulish experience and a genuine spiritual experience? What about emotionalism?

Above all, How do we "enter in"? Do we check up enough on the methodology in practice? This can be a real danger point. The way we pray for and lead people into the Spirit-filled experience is very crucial. Some of the methodology is spiritualistic and leads to the entrance of counterfeit demons.

All this calls for prayerful and careful discernment. The confusion causes many to stumble and quit. But quitting is not the answer.

We must all go back to the "drawing board" of Scripture! Be sure we are saying what *it* says—no more, no less. In the highly charged and sensitive field of the Holy Spirit, even a slight deviation from Holy Scripture can be divisive, or at least controversial.

We must find the secret of the apostles and New Testament leaders. How could they be so fully charismatic and insist on the Spirit-filled experience and life for every believer and for every church, and at the same time be equally insistent—even adamant—in not allowing splits, sectarianism, disorder and fanaticism?

We must not just dive into some experience emotionally without heartfelt preparation. And in the diversity of gifts and manifestations we must not allow divisiveness. And we must know the difference. We must not only avoid the divisiveness, but we must also find the true unity of the Spirit and insist on maintaining it. This is the apostolic secret, and it is a divine *must*.

Therefore I have set before myself a number of challenges in this book: 1) avoid extremes, 2) reconcile antagonisms, 3) discern things that differ, 4) insist on the New Testament standard of the Spirit-filled life in Christ for every believer and 5) at the same time "[endeavor] to keep the unity of the Spirit in the bond of peace" (see Ephesians 4:3).

I work with Christians and churches of all kinds; I don't want to fight anybody. I simply want to find and follow Scripture and affirm it. I have heard the Lord's new commandment: "love one another" (John 13:34).

I have lived through many years of many different spiritual experiences, many precious revivals and many different theologies and schools of thought. What concerns me is that many gifted people pay little or no attention to the fifth point I mentioned: genuine Christian *unity*. They don't want anything or anybody to come between their "letting go and letting God" lest they "quench" or "resist" or "grieve" the Holy Spirit. They are willing to stand on their heads if that is what it takes. They don't want to tell God what to do.

This is precisely the point where we differ, and where we miss the *real* point. We do not tell God what to do—true! The real point is this: *God has told us in no uncertain terms in His Word what we are to do, and what He will do.*

I often say that if we do what God tells us to do, He will do what He says He will do. That's the real answer. It's that profoundly simple. Instead, we go wild with some Scriptures and avoid other plain Scriptures which would keep us in balance.

I want to weave all five of my personal challenges listed above into the fabric of this book. And even better, I want us to see how the Lord Himself has woven them in a unified stitching throughout the New Testament.

This is perhaps the most remarkable discovery of all!

The more I search Scripture, the more I see that true Christian unity is our priority, as we shall see. Unity in Scripture is much more than doctrinal or ecclesiastical unity, though that is important too. It is a *divine* unity. And very real. It goes right back to the tri-unity in the Godhead—Father, Son and Holy Spirit. It is indeed a unity of the Spirit, and all who are born of the Spirit are in it by their new birth (John 1:12-13; chapter 3).

This is a good place to remind ourselves that all the truly great saints of the Church—filled with the Holy Spirit in great measure—are admired and almost adored. But they are not divisive or sectarian. They are ecumenical in the true sense of that word. They are the kind of people who would (as was said of Fletcher of Madley) be "a saint in any denomination." Their great spirituality drew people to the Lord. It was inviting, appealing and attractive.

And what shall we say of our Lord Jesus Christ Himself? No one on planet earth was so full of the Spirit as He. And yet He was the most unified and unifying Person who ever lived! More than anyone else He truly did "[endeavor] to keep the unity of the Spirit in the bond of peace" (Ephesians 4:3). And He was and is behind every other such endeavor—bringing all of it into being.

This is not a book on how to *live* the Spirit-filled life—it is about how to enter into it, how to get it and be sure of it, and the main differences this makes in our life with Christ.

I would really like you to have a clear answer to the great question: *Have you personally received the Holy Spirit* (to fill and empower and use you "as He wills")?

Endnote

[1] *Letters of Andrew Jukes* (New York: Longmans, Green and Co, 1903), 16.

Part 1

Filled with the Spirit:

A Fresh Approach

1

John and His Gospel

John's Gospel has brought millions to faith in Christ. Its Christology is unsurpassed, but its teaching on the Holy Spirit is equally unsurpassed.

When I began with this book I was going to let John be a kind of copilot with Paul in launching the ship into the orbit of the Spirit-filled truth and testimony. Then, the more I pursued the New Testament, the more I saw that *John* was in command of the ship when both Peter and Paul were long gone from the scene. If we follow John, he will lead us, more than any New Testament writer, in how to be filled with the Holy Spirit. The "entering in"—the starting gate experience was very much John's ministry.

Why John?

Why, we must ask, was it given to the apostle John to minister and write *last* in the New Testament?

One part of the answer must be that it was also given to him to see and to enter into what was *first*—most important—in the life of Christ.

He was the closest to Jesus: he leaned on the breast of Jesus at the Last Supper and was called the apostle whom Jesus loved. He lived on to be the oldest by far and actually had his greatest ministry when the others were long gone from the scene. He held to the original vision through thick and thin all those many years and never let it lose its luster. Everything which John writes and teaches in his Gospel about the person and work of the Holy Spirit came to his ears directly from the lips of Christ Himself. This is where John is unique.

John personalizes everyone and everything

This may well be the most unique feature in John's Gospel: All the great truths are personalized in Christ and in the Holy Spirit and come alive in different human personalities.

The *Word* is at once alive and personalized: The Word is Christ. (John 1:1)

The *new birth* is not something to be received; it is ours when we receive the person of Christ personally (1:12-13).

Eternal life is not a heavenly infusion, not something we hope to have someday by the time we die and find out if we made it to heaven—it is Christ Himself; "He who has the Son has life" (1 John 5:12).

On and on it goes like that in this great Gospel. Just think of all His great "I AMS" so diverse and so distinctive ("I am the Bread of life" . . . "I am the Good Shepherd" . . . "I am the Door" . . . "I am the Light of the world" . . . "I am the Way, the Truth and the Life" . . . "I am the Resurrection and the Life").

What are all these names? Why so many? And so diverse? They are all so many manifestations of His Person, and the works they perform are different manifestations of Himself in His glory. They are the ways in which He keeps on giving Himself away so that people of every kind may come to believe in Him. In this way John becomes the evangelist supreme, bringing many to Christ. His works are like the facets of a diamond, each reflecting the glory of Christ's Person.

The wonder of Christ's Person is that what He *is* He *does* and what He *does* He *is*. He begets. He creates. He imparts something of Himself in every one of His works. He saves us because He is the Savior. When, for example, as "the light of the world" He caused the blind man to see, He at the same time opened his eyes spiritually, so that he began to see Jesus as the Messiah (John 9).

Jesus is not only doing wonders for people. With each wonder another wonder takes place: with it He is giving Himself away and bringing people to Himself. As a Person He is dealing with people as persons and bringing them into a personal relationship with Himself.

The Holy Spirit too is always giving Himself away. He too is a real living Person. An enormous Person. Infinite. Manifold. Majestic. God in action. The executive of the Godhead. He is always giving us something new, something more, something greater of Himself and of Christ.

We are to receive Him. He fills us with Himself, not just with feelings. Sanctification, for example, is not some*thing* we receive—we are to receive *Him*, the Holy Spirit in Person, then He sanctifies. Jesus tells us it was that way with His own mighty works: "the Father who dwells in Me does the works" (14:10).

A good writer, John has a superb way of building his whole Gospel story around great personalities. The greatest of all are God the Father, God the Son and God the Holy Spirit.

Even reality is personalized. For someone as heavenly-minded as John it is magnificent to see how down-to-earth he is in his Gospel. Truth and reality are his footsteps all the way through. Jesus is the Truth. And truth in John also means reality. The same is true of the Holy Spirit: He is the Spirit of Truth.

The truth of Christ becomes reality in those whom John presents. John is never vague. The Way, the Truth and the Life are all personalized in Christ and at once become real in those who find and receive Him.

And in writing all this, John spreads his own personality and experience throughout. All flow, like rivers, out of his own innermost being by the Holy Spirit. He experienced just what Jesus had promised (see 7:38).

This is his way of constantly personalizing and magnifying and glorifying the Person of Christ. It is his way of revealing just who

Christ *is* and what He *does*. His words and works unite as an indivisible flame, ignited in his innermost being by the Person of the Holy Spirit. What a Gospel!

We do not just come to Christ asking for His salvation: we receive Him personally (person-to-Person). In doing so we are not only saved, but we *have eternal life. He* is that Life.

That is also true of the Holy Spirit. He is God, to be sure. But He is also a Person to be received and known, just as we received Christ. The same word "receive" used for our receiving *Christ* is used of receiving the *Holy Spirit*. There are two distinct Persons, but each is received in a similar fashion.

Seer supreme of the New Testament

Like an eagle, John soars and sees above others. He can see the Sun of righteousness above and at the same time spot his prey below. In his writings he does not merely fight an error such as gnosticism—he swiftly pounces on it. He observes with eyesight, insight, foresight and hindsight. His foresight tells us things which are to come and his hindsight tells us things which Jesus said would come—all by the insight of the same Spirit who filled him.

When it comes to having clear focus and vision concerning Christ and the Church, the two major doctrines of the New Testament, he has twenty-twenty vision. He sees both.

As a born-again believer he sees the kingdom of God. He enters into it, and it enters into him by the Holy Spirit (John 3).

To him the miracles of Jesus were *signs;* he could see Jesus in them revealed as the Christ (Messiah), the Son of God, bringing people to faith and eternal life through Him (20:30-31).

Finally, to him the visions of the book of Revelation were given. There he reveals the last things of Christ: His judgments, beginning at the house of God (the churches) and extending over the earth, all centered at the throne of God and heading up into the coming again of Christ Himself.

He seldom mentions his name, yet he is by no means anonymous. He hides his person in that of Jesus. And because he and Jesus are so much one he often gives scholars a workout to tell which are the words of John and which are the words of Jesus. But in this we get to see and know him fully.

All this and more came into being because he was filled with the Holy Spirit.

Why did John outlast the other apostles? One reason was that by living so long he could recall to us that which was first. He is now the only one who could say of every movement of the New Testament—from John the Baptist to Jesus to Pentecost to the many churches of the New Testament and finally to Ephesus and all the churches founded in Asia by Paul—*I was there.*

He knew most of the others, what they said, taught, experienced and wrote.

Above all, he was the closest to Jesus, and what he writes about Jesus is mostly what he heard directly from Jesus. This is perhaps the most unique thing about his Gospel. It is mostly made up of the words and works which came directly from Jesus.

As we read we think we are listening to John; but we are really listening to Jesus. Actually, we know we are listening to Jesus—to the life of Jesus now living in John.

He could not sing it yet, but he could say it:

> I was there when they crucified my
>   Lord . . .
> sometimes it causes me to tremble . . .
>   tremble . . . tremble.

I was there when they laid Him in
the tomb. . . .
I was there when God raised Him
from the grave. . . .

"I was there when for forty days He kept on
showing Himself alive to us by many infallible
proofs, speaking things about the kingdom of
God which He had never made known before
in all our three years with Him.

"How well do I remember the first day I met
Jesus. How could I ever forget it! It was at
John the Baptist's Jordan River camp meeting.
I was already a disciple of John. One day Jesus
was walking nearby and John pointed to Him:
'Behold the Lamb of God!' (John 1:36). At
once I began to follow Jesus, and became His
disciple. Yes, *I was there.*

"I must also tell you about the last day I was
with Jesus. It was His last day on earth. We
disciples were all back in Jerusalem again, and
we thought, *This could be the time for Him to
set up His great kingdom on earth!*

"He is now the *resurrected* Lord Jesus Christ
and has a new, glorified spiritual body. Even
the Romans can't undo Him anymore.

"But we were all startled and taken by surprise when suddenly, right before our eyes He

was lifted up from the earth and ascended—to be enthroned on high.

"We had to rethink everything!"

It all happened (His birth, life, words, works, death, resurrection, ascension) by the same Holy Spirit who filled Him, "above measure" and above all others, at the time He was baptized by John at the Jordan River.

John could say as no other disciple could: "I was well acquainted with Peter, Paul and Luke and their many ministries and writings. I also knew Mark, for it was in his mother's home we all prayed together and at Pentecost saw the gathering turn into the very first New Testament Church.

"Not only did I know about those churches in Asia which Paul established and how they all functioned in the power of the Holy Spirit; I *was there* in those same churches some years later, leading and overseeing them as God's apostle. Even after many had fallen away, I heard the Lord call them to repent. They were to light up their cities for God as they did in the days of their first love (see Revelation 1-3).

"All through those years, with all our many ups and downs and differences and diversity of

22

gifts and manifold ministries, I must tell you (says John), we all agreed on our message and the way we should lead our churches to be filled with the Holy Spirit. We even used the same formula, which we got from the mouth of Jesus Himself. And we got the same results as He did when He breathed on us and said, 'Receive the Holy Spirit.'

"From the early days, and all through the years I was involved in this ministry with Christ. *I was there.*"

And now he is John the aged. In him we have a good example that last is not least. By this time he is worth his weight in gold as a leader of the New Testament.

John is more than an eyewitness

It is easy to see that throughout his Gospel John is an eyewitness. An eyewitness is powerful in any court; we are told that one good witness is worth twenty lawyers.

But John is also an ear-witness, for he heard every word from Jesus Himself.

That is not all, for with and beneath all his words John is telling us what is taking place in his own life. This is what is so unique about the Gospel of John.

His own personality permeates every chapter. In a hidden way he is telling us his own inner journey with Christ: how he received Him personally, how he received the Holy Spirit personally and entered the life of His fullness—in short, his own life *with* Christ as well as his life *in* Christ.

John did not have to think up his story. The fact that he wrote last is another way of telling us that his Gospel is full of scenes and events which he had preached and taught and discipled in the churches for at least two generations of ministry. And now, at last—urged perhaps by many elders—he wrote it all in the form of the Gospel of John. He probably did not know that you and I and millions of others would read it and come face-to-face with Jesus through his Gospel.

John and Jesus are so close that we can almost hear the heartbeat of Jesus. John found himself fully by fully losing his life fully in Christ. John is never more himself and never more fulfilled than when he is filled with the Spirit of Jesus. This is also God's way for us.

John clears up confusion

In a day when there is a lot of confusion about the way we are to be filled with the Holy

Spirit and what is to result when we are filled, John comes to the front with clear and inspired answers.

We must be very clear in how we lead people into the Spirit-filled life. Some of the techniques practiced today are more like spiritualism and lead to demonic experiences. I have in mind seeking manifestations and doing so in a spirit of passivity: "just let yourself go" . . . "let your mind go blank" . . . "seek tongues" . . . "let God have full control of your being," etc.

God's way is the way of faith—living faith. Faith that comes by way of full obedience: "the obedience of faith."

What then is to be the real result? Here again, John makes it clear: the real result is found in the word *"sonship."* That means full submission and obedience—complete filial dependence on the Father, just as it was for Christ Himself.

Have you noticed, in John, how Jesus refers everything to the Father? Where we might expect Him to say the Holy Spirit was working, He says the work was all through "the Father." This tells us something. The triune God is never divided, but it really is the Holy Spirit who does it all, for He is the executive—the One who carries out the actions—of the Godhead.

A New Thing

*P*lease, first read John 13-16 several times. Here Jesus brings us into a "new thing": His famous "upper room discourse" spoken the night before His crucifixion. This is the "holy place" in John's Gospel. Only Christ's own are present; they were already full-fledged disciples with a great track record, having evangelized all of Galilee in the north.

Now Jesus has them all to Himself for a "new thing" before He would be crucified and rise again from the dead. It is very likely the same upper room where these very words would soon be fulfilled at Pentecost. Scholars tell us it probably was the house of Mary, the mother of Mark, the house where the first New Testament Church was born.

Here are some of the things which will be "new":

- Jesus now gives His "new commandment": Christians are to love one another. This will take care of most of the problems in the new Church (John 13).

- The new "day" will be the day of the Holy Spirit at Pentecost, a day which would characterize this age and become God's "new age movement," a day and age when Spirit-filled churches are to be planted for worldwide evangelization.

- Jesus gives many new promises: They are to 1) have a new prayer life—much larger, with much greater answers—when they pray in His name. 2) And they are to have a new and much greater life in the Holy Spirit. 3) He will fill them, and through them bring conviction of sin and conversions to Christ in a much deeper and greater and more powerful way (John 16).

- Jesus tells us that in His Father's house are many mansions, and that He is going to prepare a place for us. But in the same chapter He tells us that *we* are His mansion for His indwelling "down here" (14:2, 23).

  In other words, there is no need for us to hurry to heaven, because He brought the eternal, abiding, abundant life of heaven *here*, in His own Person. We can say it like this: Jesus brought the hereafter here, so now that is what we are after here!

- We are to have a new and much more fruitful life: not only are we to *pick* fruit, but we are to *bear* fruit—lots of it. We are to pray it into being, to birth it as Jesus did (John 15).

You can see how we must give our full attention to these chapters: first, because only John gives us these words of Jesus; second, with this discourse Jesus gives us something very full and final concerning the Spirit-filled Christian life. I should hasten to say He takes us away from anything shallow or wild or superficial. John stabilizes what too often turns into imbalance and extremes.

This is one of the unique features of John's Gospel: he clarifies, amplifies, solidifies and simplifies—and the glories of Christ fill those whom He fills with His Spirit.

John 17

Now we enter the "holiest of all" in John's

Gospel. Jesus, our great High Priest, opens the veil by opening up His whole inner being in a final prayer of intercession. Nowhere else does He open it all up like this; He waits to the very end to do it. And He does it in prayer. Why? Because His whole life was a life of prayer and answered prayer.

It sounds strange, but nothing in His life was original: all was given from the Father in prayer. This is what was original with Jesus: His enormous and glorious prayer life.

He opens up to us through this prayer all that has been flowing through Him from His own Spirit-filled being.

He lets us see into His innermost being, and tells us that everything in His life (words, works, men, etc.) came from His Father, and in answer to His praying. He did not *do* things; he *prayed* everything into being. What a prayer life!

And, would you believe it, all is communicable and transferable for us too! He models it all. That's the way it was with Jesus: He did not just pray *about things*, He *brought things about by prayer*.

The disciples had no idea just then that everything they had seen at work through Him would soon be at work in them! He would be *in them* doing it. How I love the closing three words of this great prayer: *"I in them . . ."* (17:26).

As Jesus prays He spells out precisely what it all is which had been at work in Him and which, when answered, would be at work in them . . . and in us:

- His *keeping* power. This is no small matter. (17:12)
- His *joy*. Yes, not any kind of joy, but *His* joy. (17:13)
- His *Word*. We are to live by it, as He did. (17:14)
- His *sanctification*. Our true separation from the world. (17:17, 19)
- His *service* in sending us. Just as the Father sent Him. (17:18)
- His *disciples*. All were given from the Father. All were answers to prayer. (17:6)
- And His kind of *unity*. (17:21-22)

Here He brings us to the epicenter of the whole prayer: Christian *unity*. Like never before in Scripture, we see what kind of unity the Lord has in mind for His Church: not ecumenical or even doctrinal unity is as important as the Lord's idea of unity. It is a new and organic unity; it is unique *oneness*—the very same oneness which He has with His Father.

Jesus prays for it five times (emphasis added each time):

1. "That they may be *one* as We are" (17:11)
2. "That they all may be *one,* as You, Father, are in Me, and I in You" (17:21)
3. "That they also may be *one* in Us" (17:21)
4. "That they may be made perfect in *one*" (17:23)
5. "The glory which You gave Me I have given them, that they may be *one* just as We are one" (17:22).

Notice all the new things which are to come from this new oneness:

- His *glory* is bound up with it and is communicated with it. I once thought that "when we die we'll get to glory." But here we see that Jesus can and does communicate it *here*. And that is given in connection with this loving oneness. In every great revival the Holy Spirit comes like this—in glory. That is one way of describing what happens in the glorious atmosphere of a real revival.

- In that way, and in that oneness, many come to *believe* in Christ (17:20). It really brings the Church into a new, more powerful kind of evangelism and soul-winning. Short of it we may win people to Christ; but in a powerful revival there is a special mark on the converts: both in quality and in quantity.

- Through this kind of oneness people not only come to believe, but they also come to know that the Father sent Jesus (17:23). If I may say so, this is a kind of "scientific evidence" the world recognizes as genuine Christianity. Jesus said this also: "By this all will *know* that you are My disciples, if you have love for one another" (13:35, emphasis added).

Every doctrine is alive and well and personalized in Christ. All is organic. There is not an organizational word in the whole prayer.

Praying to stay on

In short, Jesus is not so much praying to leave us as He is praying to stay on . . . live on

. . . live His life in His people, His new body, His new Church.

This high priestly prayer of Jesus is perhaps the greatest prayer in all Scripture, and we should get on our knees with it again and again. It is a very down-to-earth prayer, meant to be answered and experienced by us down here.

Was it answered? I should say it was! Not only was it answered, but it was answered in detail—answered to the very letter by the Spirit. And it demonstrates how fully prayer can be answered and what it can accomplish here on earth.

The book of Acts takes us to the answer in just a few weeks. When we see just how it was all answered, we are further awed. As so often with God's great answers, we have to say, "Who would have thought it would be answered like that?"

A New Kind of Unity

In John 17 Jesus prays five times for this loving oneness. In the book of Acts (the book of the Church) we read of this new kind of unity five times. The word—a new word which Luke uses for it and may even have coined—is *homothumadon*, translated "with one accord."

1. "These all [about 120] continued *with one accord* in prayer and supplication, with the women and Mary the mother of Jesus, and with His brothers" (Acts 1:14, emphasis added). In John 17 Jesus was praying this first New Testament prayer meeting into being. Forty days before, at the time of His crucifixion, His disciples forsook Him and fled. It seemed to be all over!

But *He* was not finished! As the resurrected Christ, He revived them all and built them together into His new Church in the form of a prayer meeting. What a revelation!

2. "When the Day of Pentecost had fully come, they were all *with one accord* in one place" (Acts 2:1, emphasis added). Joseph Parker of London called this the greatest possible unity on earth.

The Church was all united before Pentecost. And that is precisely one of the conditions for such fullness of the Spirit.

3. "And they, continuing *daily with one accord* in the temple, and breaking bread from house to house, did eat their meat with gladness and singleness of heart" (2:46, KJV, emphasis added).

There was now a church of at least 3,120

members. And they were *all* with one accord. That means the original "one accord" unity continued as the basic secret for its ongoing growth and power and advancement in the Spirit. It also tells us that new converts can blend right in and at once become a part of the Church's great oneness. This is just the way it is when churches come into precious "reviving again."

Acts, let us remember, does not reveal some special or abnormal kind of Church life; it reveals God's norm. When we depart from it, we must repent and return to it. This is what revival praying is all about.

4. The whole Jerusalem congregation—thousands of them—"lifted up their voice to God *with one accord*" again in a massive prayer meeting (4:24, KJV, emphasis added). They all prayed for new boldness and power and signs and wonders in the name of Jesus and in the face of enormous opposition. "The place where they were assembled together was shaken; and they were all filled with the Holy Spirit" (4:31) again. And now we are told that "the multitude of those who believed *were of one heart and one soul;* . . . they had all things in common" (4:32, emphasis added). The original Pentecostal power

seemed now to be greater than ever! The oneness secret continued.

5. "And through the hands of the apostles many signs and wonders were done among the people. And they were *all with one accord* in Solomon's Porch" (5:12, emphasis added).

This was right after two sudden funerals, when Ananias and Sapphira were suddenly stricken in death for "lying to the Holy Spirit." The Holy Spirit would not allow their lying spirit to break up the Church's unity. This judgment miracle brought new awe. People hardly dared to join that Church now; and yet there were more "joiners" than ever, for we read that "believers were increasingly added to the Lord, *multitudes* of both men and women" (5:14, emphasis added). And miracles continued.

We must not forget, either, that we have now seen the two great results Jesus had prayed for: people would come to believe in Christ and would come to know Him.

The way John 17 was prayed and answered in Acts should quicken and renew us all in prayer and in our desire to be filled with the Holy Spirit.

Christ Manifests the Glory of God

The Shekinah glory (the manifest Presence of God) which rested over the tabernacle of Moses and miraculously led God's people for forty years as a cloudy pillar by day and a pillar of fire by night now rested on Jesus. John writes: "The Word was made flesh, and dwelt [tabernacled] among us, (and we beheld his glory, the glory as of the only begotten of the Father,) full of grace and truth" (John 1:14, KJV). All through the Gospel of John we behold this glory in Christ—in His mighty works, in His death and resurrection and finally in His ascension when "a cloud received Him out of their sight" as they were intently watching (Acts 1:9).

This glory can also be imparted to us. In John 17 Jesus prays, "And the glory which You [Father] gave Me I have given them" (John 17:22). In fact, this glory is involved in all that He prays to be given here.

It is this glory which filled His new Church at Pentecost and is to rest on the Church and churches until He comes again. This is the way the apostle Paul prays when he prays for "glory in the church by Christ Jesus throughout all ages, world without end. Amen" (Ephesians 3:21, KJV).

When churches lose this glory, they need to be revived. Then it returns.

A Bi-level Gospel

John's Gospel reflects the bi-level life of John himself. These are the two levels or layers in the life of Christ and of our life in Christ. And it is given to John to reveal these with great clarity and simplicity:

1. Chapters 1-12 cover our "eternal life" in various ways, scene after scene (life *of* Christ).

2. Chapters 13-16 uncover how Christ now will go *deeper* and *inward* by the filling of the Holy Spirit. The Christ *for and before* them will become the Christ *in them* (life *in* Christ).

I'm sure Peter and John and the others had no idea that this wonderful Christ who was doing all these wonders would one day be living His life in them! He was now not so much preparing to leave them in John 17 as He was preparing to stay on and live on in them. That new "day" (as He also called it) was upon them—the Day of Pentecost and the new way of life, all by the Holy Spirit.

That would be for them, and for us, the new wonder!

John also expresses this twofold Christian life like this:

- "Life eternal" becomes "abiding and abundant life"
- "Spring of living water" becomes "rivers of living water"
- "Person of Christ" is received . . . "Person of the Holy Spirit" is received.

Note, too, how John uses the same word "receive" for both. And he in no way confuses the two Persons.

We have to say that John, like no other, clarifies the way we are to enter into the life *of* Christ and the full life *in* Christ. John is the evangelist, leading millions to believe in and receive Christ personally and become Christians, and he is also the revivalist, leading believers and churches into the Spirit-filled Christian life.

No wonder the Eastern church calls John the theologian of the New Testament.

Never Change Your Center

This bi-level Gospel does not mean that John

now shifts his center from Christ to the Holy Spirit. Some strong Spirit-filled experiences tend to do that, and it quickly leads to big problems, controversies, splits and often other "isms."

John does not allow any such sectarianism— not by fighting it but by affirming his great Word on the Holy Spirit.

If we suddenly shift our center from Christ to the Holy Spirit, we are not centered. (How many centers do we need? If we have more than one center we are eccentric!) If Christ unites, what in the world should ever divide us?

For John the Spirit-filled Christian is more centered than ever—in Christ. Actually, we don't know Christ in full until we are filled with His Spirit.

We Must Keep the Unity of the Spirit

The primary concern of the apostle Paul was the same as that of Jesus and John. He expressed it in very strong language: "endeavoring to keep the unity of the Spirit in the bond of peace" (Ephesians 4:3).

I've already written about the profound unity which Christ prayed for in John 17 and how it was answered in the Acts. Now the same burden rests on Paul, and he never lets it get away from him, though his many churches (yes,

Spirit-filled churches) test him to the limit on it. Each church has its own way of endangering this unity of the Spirit. The reason that did not happen was that Paul set up a strict watch to prevent it. So must we.

He *endeavored* to keep that unity in the bond of peace. The word "endeavor" is a strong word. It literally means "make every effort" to do it. In short, give it your undivided attention . . . and effort. We could say "work hard at it." Do we do that? Paul did. "Spare no effort to make fast with bonds of peace the unity which the Spirit gives" (literal translation).

All Paul's epistles express his strong effort at keeping that unity—a unity he knows he does not *make,* but which he must *keep.* No person or church body makes Christian unity. Who do we think we are? That is a work of God, a work of the Holy Spirit—a unity we are born into when we are born again of the same Holy Spirit. It takes some half a lifetime to learn that not one of us can *make* that unity. It seems that council after council has been saddled on the Church to find the secret and the basis for true Christian unity.

When we are born again, we wake up to see that we have it! Then we really go to work, with Christ, to *keep* it.

Back to Paul again. It seems to me that he is endeavoring to keep the unity in all his many epistles. It comes through in his letter to the church in Rome. It crescendoes in Romans 12 and sounds out in verse 16: "Be of the same mind toward one another." Even before that, he says the Jews will also be one with the Gentiles again: they will be grafted back into the one original olive tree (Romans 11).

With the highly gifted Corinthian congregation—full of a party spirit and ready for splits—Paul wastes no time zeroing in on this concern. In the very first chapter he writes in no uncertain terms:

> Now I plead with you, brethren, by the name of our Lord Jesus Christ, that you all speak the same thing, and that there be no divisions among you, but that you be perfectly joined together in the same mind and in the same judgment. (1 Corinthians 1:10)

The Galatian church, filled with the Holy Spirit, was getting back into legalism with it. Another divisive spirit. With them Paul guards the unity of the Spirit by upholding their freedom through the Spirit.

The Thessalonian church was getting unbalanced by some extreme views of Christ's second advent. This congregation had not only had the gospel preached to them, but it had been preached in the power and demonstration of the Spirit (1 Thessalonians 1:5). Even with all that, they needed careful watching and monitoring to avoid extremes and divisiveness.

These churches challenged and stretched the great apostle to the limit in his stance for keeping the power and the unity of the Spirit together in the bond of peace.

Even his dear Philippian congregation was facing trouble. A rift was developing. Two women, Euodia and Syntyche, were at odds and probably not wanting even to speak to each other. Paul nips this spirit in the bud. He writes clearly: "I implore Euodia and I implore Syntyche to be of the same mind in the Lord" (Philippians 4:2).

Then when we come to Ephesians, a later writing, he "lets it all out," giving us at last the binding and bonding secret which was his constant methodology from the first with every church: "endeavoring to keep the unity of the Spirit in the bond of peace" (4:3).

Jesus never sectarianizes, though a lot of it is done by us in His name. There is not a drop of sectarian blood in Him!

He makes one division, and only one. That division is in *Him* . . . His own person. He makes that clear: "He who is not with Me is against Me" (Matthew 12:30); "So there was a division among the people because of *Him*" (John 7:43; see also 9:16; 10:19).

Jesus does not split churches or separate Christians from Christians. He does separate Christians from others, but in such a way that they love non-Christians not less but more, as He does. In His Person He has and is the whole unifying plan of God in His Church. Yes, even in the whole cosmos (see Ephesians 1).

Jesus brings people to Jesus! And the more we have of His Spirit, the more we have of Him. We are to "grow up in all things into Him who is the head—Christ" (Ephesians 4:15). He is our unifying center, our circumference, our all in all. If we follow His way into the filling of the Spirit, we'll get "the real thing" and at the same time stay out of trouble and divisiveness.

What is His way? What is His "methodology" for getting us "in"? I'll major in this answer in later chapters; but let me say this much here. He says: "Blessed are those who hunger and thirst for righteousness, for they shall be *filled*" (Matthew 5:6, emphasis added).

That verse alone (and there are many more) will steer us aright.

I have lived through the many danger zones of divisiveness and sectarianism. Somewhere I learned these lines, and I love them:

> Because you belong to Christ,
>   You are akin to me;
> One in the bonds unbreakable,
>   Wrought for eternity.
> Spirit with spirit joined,
>   Who can those ties undo?
> Binding the Christ within my heart
>   Unto the Christ in You.
>   (Anonymous)

John Fits between Luke and Acts

There may be more than one reason why John's Gospel is located after Luke and right before Acts. Luke and Acts, both written by Luke, are perfect companions (see Acts 1:1), but John comes right between them. Does John spoil their continuity? Not at all. Rather, his Gospel enlarges on it and clarifies what

46

could otherwise be a gap. In short, John's account of the Holy Spirit becomes a part of the continuity.

John takes us to the upper room where Jesus tells all about the Holy Spirit they all should know and were to receive. Then he tells us just how and when and where the Spirit was to be received—right there, in the same upper room and through the mouth and lips of Jesus Himself.

With John's story in mind, we are really ready for Luke's account when we open up the book of Acts, the book of the Church—the *Spirit-filled* Church.

3

The Holy Spirit and
His Manifestations

What about manifestations of the Spirit in the Church?

This is where the rubber meets the road. It is when we seek the gifts and manifestations of the Spirit that we have our problems, especially if we seek the gift of tongues. There are problems even with the best of Holy Spirit manifestations, but only with the seekers—not with the Holy Spirit.

We are like the man who said he has a lot of music in him, but it spoils on the way out.

It is when the Person of the Holy Spirit comes through us and our person that the manifestation takes place. And the change.

The word "manifestation" itself means that *He* comes into action, is seen and on display.

That's when the "music" begins. It can be beautiful, it can spoil on the way out and it can even be bad. Even at best the music is no longer 100 percent Holy Spirit. It is also 100 percent *me—my* person. And the music depends on how perfectly we blend together.

The original symphony, the 120-member orchestra of believers in Acts, were "all with one accord" on the Day of Pentecost (Acts 2:1). They were in perfect harmony when the Spirit filled them, and the music they manifested in those first chapters is some of the most beautiful and joyful we can hear.

The Holy Spirit music was different in Paul's church at Corinth. Their gifts were spoiling it on the way out. They needed plenty of discernment, control and correction.

The Pentecost Church was different (Acts 2). It was in full harmony. It set the standard for churches. They were no longer babes; they had been tried and tested, having gone through every kind of temptation with Jesus. They were seasoned with salt and proven.

Their gift of tongues may have sounded the same as at Corinth, but there was a difference in manifestation. At Pentecost they were full and effective because they had been tried and tested in all *His* testings and temptations, and were now mature. They needed no one to test out their new "tongues" manifestations to find out if they were genuine. Their new "tongues speaking" was in the languages and even dialects of the many nationalities gathered in Jerusalem from the Mediterranean world; they brought about the conviction which, along with Peter's great preaching, brought about 3,000 to faith in Christ—all on the same day. All were Jews. That takes power: If you don't think so, just try to get even one Jew converted to Christ!

Manifestations differ greatly, especially in the way we seek them. In fact, we should not even seek manifestations. Why not? Because it can be dangerous. It is putting the cart before the horse.

Question: Does "not seeking" manifestations mean there will be no manifestations?

Indeed not. The opposite is true: there will be all kinds of them. The apostle Paul lists them in First Corinthians 12, and the apostle John gives us the last word written about them in his Gospel.

The very idea of a *filling* is a manifestation. All the many and varied charismata of the Spirit are manifestations. *But they are not the way into this fullness. They are not the gift of the Spirit Himself.* Even when they accompany the infilling, they are distinct and function as distinct manifestations.

Question: If we do not seek these gifts, how will we get them? How are they given and received?

This is where the apostle Paul instructs us. He lists them in First Corinthians 12, calls them "manifestations" and tells us how they are given and received. He writes:

> But the manifestation of the Spirit is given to each one for the profit of all: for to one is given the *word of wisdom* through the Spirit, to another the *word of knowledge* through the same Spirit, to another *faith* by the same Spirit, to another *gifts of healings* by the same Spirit, to another the *working of miracles,* to another *prophecy,* to another *discerning of spirits,* to another *different kinds of tongues,* to another the *interpretation*

of tongues. But one and the same Spirit works all these things, distributing to each one individually *as He wills*. (12:7-11, emphasis added)

In other words, these gifts are separate manifestations. He sovereignly controls them and gives to each one separately and distinctly and differently as He wills. *We pray for and receive the gift of the Spirit Himself,* and when we do, He gives these gifts ("gracious bestowments") *as He wills*.

When my brothers and sisters and I were children, at Christmastime we eagerly awaited grandmother's big box, full of gifts for each of us. We could hardly wait, wondering what our gift would be. Each was different, carefully wrapped and marked. We would always be surprised and full of joy, for each gift was well planned and well suited for each of us. The big package was the gift; with it came all the individual gifts. The Holy Spirit Himself is the gift, and with Him come His gifts, well marked and ready and suited for each of us in the Spirit.

Pentecost

Question: What about Pentecost? Didn't they all receive the gift of tongues?

Yes, indeed they did. But (and here is where we have to be most careful) they did not *seek* tongues. They are manifestations—not mandates. Paul later makes it clear that not all speak with tongues (12:30).

None of the prayerful seekers had any idea of the way the Holy Spirit would work and manifest Himself. No one had a mental picture of what was coming, or if he did, it certainly was not the way he thought.

The Lord never used that kind of technique as evidence. Any of the many accompanying gifts were evidences, and they had them all. But none was ever singled out in Scripture as the main one.

The gift of tongues was given, but not sought. It was just one of the gifts which Paul mentions in First Corinthians 12. They were all there, given in the same way: "as He wills" and exactly as Paul later taught in First Corinthians 12.

Our Methodology

All this gets us into something very basic and primary, and that is our *methodology*. Just how do we teach and preach and lead people into this high and holy experience of being filled with the Spirit of God?

This is truly important, and this is where trouble begins if we let go of the Word of God, and just "let go and let God" in our seeking. To be totally abandoned to God does not mean we must recklessly abandon ourselves. A lot of wild and extreme things are happening to people who seek this way. We do not find "abandoning ourselves" as a way to be filled in Scripture.

We must not, for example, dash into some experience of tongues, and then later have to test this out to see if we have the real gift. This is not the scriptural way.

The right way is to prepare our hearts, repent, be cleansed of any known sin . . . then come to God's altar in full surrender, full obedience and in simple faith receive—not tongues, but the Holy Spirit *Himself*.

A lot of praying for the Holy Spirit is passive, even spiritualistic, and leads to demonic demonstrations and manifestations. If we heed God's Word and go God's way, Satan cannot get in. The closest he can get is to observe.

Further Thoughts on Controls

"Tongues," for example, are prominent in the New Testament churches, but never dominant. They never are allowed to take control—they need to be kept *under* control. Many gifted believers learn this the hard way. And if they are not humble and teachable here, they have more problems.

I know many who have a genuine gift of tongues; but they have learned to obey God's Word and learned about His controls. The result is they not only continue in the church "endeavoring to keep the unity of the Spirit in the bond of peace" (Ephesians 4:3), but have become strong intercessors helping to bring revival and strong witnessing power to the congregation.

The Difference the Spirit-filled Life Makes

Let us look at what comes in focus fully when we are filled with His Spirit:

- The "spring of water" which was in us "springing up unto eternal life" (John 4) now suddenly becomes "rivers of living water." Not just *a* river, but rivers (plural). They flow from the same inner being, now called "our innermost being" (John 7).

  (John always emphasizes the inward . . . not only the ingoing but the outgoing, and outflowing from within. He also avoids at once the danger of wrong introspection. Our eyes are not turning in, but are on Him, away from self: "he that believes on me, as the Scripture says" is the way here.)

- Eternal life, which we have in Christ, becomes His abiding and abundant life. Abiding in Him we bear fruit . . . much fruit . . . more fruit. (John 15 also relates this to the "greater work" of the Holy Spirit.)

- We received Christ . . . now we receive the Holy Spirit. They are not the same and are not confused in John's Gospel. Christ was resident, and so was the Holy Spirit (who gave us Christ). Now Christ gives us the Holy Spirit, who in a real sense becomes "president," carrying out the work of God. But the Holy Spirit in turn makes Christ full and complete and Lord of all, in control of the house He has already lived in, in complete control now of every room in us.

- We have a fully God-controlled, Spirit-led lifestyle. The first thing in Jesus' own experience was complete guidance by the Father. He was the role model of *sonship* as demonstrated in Matthew 4 and Luke 4. So sonship (not just gifts, important as they are) is the real test and result of our being filled with the Spirit. This cannot be overemphasized. A full prayer life and a full life of living by the Word of Scripture showed up at once when Jesus received the Spirit in definite and full measure.

In Romans 8:14 we learn that "as many as are led by the Spirit of God, these are sons of God"—not mere babes, but sons come of age. So, if sonship is the big new mark of the Spirit-fullness, guidance is the great mark of our full sonship.

You and I are no longer on our own, because we no longer *are* our own. We live the exchanged life, His life in ours and our life in His. It is an obedient life, submissive, fully filial and dependent, a life where He not only takes charge of our "spiritual" life, but *all* of our life and living. Everything now is spiritual. And all of it is now on a prayer basis, just as it was with Jesus, who not only prayed about everything, but who brought everything about by prayer. A whole new prayer life dawns on us and opens up to us.

If we have a church full of such people, as Jesus planned and actually brought into being when He built His Church in Jerusalem, wonderful things happen. All by the same Holy Spirit.

Must All Speak with Tongues?

The Day of Pentecost

It is clear from Acts 2 that all who were filled with the Spirit on the Day of Pentecost did speak with tongues. And most uniquely in the languages and even dialects of the many nationalities present from all lands for the great feast of Pentecost.

But to say that therefore all *must* speak with tongues is going beyond Scripture, and at once creates a problem—making the tongues into a new "unity"—or, more precisely, into a new divisiveness or sectarianism.

A closer look into Scripture ("the drawing board") corrects it all and keeps the true unity of the Spirit. There is no mandate there for speaking with tongues. There are some mighty mandates (such as the Great Commission), and we must heed those. It is clear that on the Day of Pentecost the gift of tongues accompanied the baptism and filling of the Holy Spirit—but so did all the other gifts of the

Spirit. So why single out the tongues? Because they surfaced and were the most ecstatic gifts.

But what about the other gifts like wisdom and faith, gifts which were more important but nondivisive? No one ever shouts "Hallelujah" for the exercise and manifestation of the gift of wisdom or faith.

The apostles were given *all* the special gifts at Pentecost—and not by seeking any of them. They received the Holy Spirit Himself, and then *He* sovereignly divided these gifts "as He wills." The experience was the same at Pentecost as it was later in Paul's description and teaching in First Corinthians 12.

The Apostle Paul

When the Holy Spirit, the Gift Himself, divides the gifts separately "as He wills," there is no divisiveness! Some of the Corinthian Christians may have wanted to press tongues on the others. But the apostle Paul would not allow it. He held them to the unity of the Spirit. They were about to split on various things. The apostle clearly discerns one danger when he asks, "Do all speak with tongues?" The answer is "no," supported in the Greek text. And we must not manipulate Scripture to another point of view.

The apostle insists that there is to be "no schism [split] in the body" (12:25).

To be filled with the Spirit should deepen, not divide, the unity we have in Christ.

John

The Gospel of John clarifies matters fully. John is deeply devoted both to unity and to the Spirit. Like Paul, John endeavors to keep the unity of the Spirit in the bond of peace.

He does not even mention tongues, though he personally received the gift along with the others at Pentecost and gives us as full a menu of the Spirit's fullness and ministry as any others.

Not only does John write last, but he writes what has outlasted different views. John is still the standard bearer of what was standard apostolic teaching and practice. His language had now become standard in New Testament practice.

Though he differs from Paul in the way he presents Spirit-filled truth and testimony, he does not differ in the way we enter into it or in what happens when we do. Dare we say that Jesus was not filled with the Holy Spirit because He did not speak in tongues? Dare we even say that the great saints of the Church were not filled with the Spirit because they did not speak with tongues? When we do this we grieve the Holy Spirit and break up the unity we were told to keep.

John avoids all this. Yet no one is more plain or profound in revealing the Person and work of the Holy Spirit in the life of believers.

Further Thought on the Gift of Tongues

The gift of tongues accompanied the downpour and overflow of the Holy Spirit on the Day of Pentecost, but the gift was never sent or meant to become a bottleneck. The Spirit was not meant to flow through the tongues; they were part of the flow from the Spirit.

A sign? Yes. But not *the* sign; there were others. They were signs *following*, not *leading*. They were signs for the unbeliever, not the believer.

Pentecost did not create another unity; it deepened the unity ("one accord") which was already there—organic—and fully functioning in prayer (Acts 1:14).

Tongues must not divide Christians. They were never meant to be a deciding gift. Distinctive, yes; divisive, no! The tongues were prominent, but never dominant. They have not even now united Spirit-filled Christians.

Why not? Because they were never given to unite—they were given to those who were united in Christ. If Christians are not united before they receive the Holy Spirit, they can become even more divisive. Tongues never brought unity and have never kept it. True Christian unity centers in Christ and in all who are in Christ.

The gift of tongues is a wonderful gift of God when it is right. We've had lots of it in our revival meetings in Norway, and it may surprise you to hear they were not part of the Pentecostal movement. But in my many years of experience I have not found those who speak with tongues to be more spiritual or powerful or fine-tuned than those who were filled with the Spirit and did not speak with tongues. Tongues are not the great criteria; it is the total life of the Spirit and the total life of Christ which tells.

The important thing is to receive the Holy Spirit and get to know Him as a Person. He speaks, and He can speak to you. Jesus said: "My sheep *hear My voice*, and . . . follow Me" (John 10:27, emphasis added); "they do not know the voice of strangers" (10:5).

It would be sad indeed if we could only hear His voice through the speaking in tongues.

That would at once eliminate the great saints of God who have helped to change the face of humanity. It would sectarianize the work of the Holy Spirit, limiting His speaking to tongues-speaking.

The day is coming, I believe, when such divisiveness will disappear. It is not in Scripture. Why should we have it?

Spirit-filled: What Is the Best Evidence?

No writer is clearer on this than John. He puts the more-than-fully gifted Christ before us all the way through his Gospel.

We know that Jesus was anointed with the Spirit above His fellows (see Hebrews 1:9). And John tells us that to Him the Spirit was given "not . . . by measure" (John 3:34). Filled with the Spirit, Jesus did not suddenly become a superman, acting on His own. The opposite is the truth. He never was more dependent on His Father for His life and messianic ministry. He says it very plainly: "I can of Myself do nothing" (5:19, author's paraphrase). Though He possessed the Holy Spirit and all His powers in supreme measure and did the mighty works that no other man ever did, He never made power the deciding factor. This is very instructive. "Though He was a Son, yet He learned obedience by the things which He suffered" (Hebrews 5:8).

His blessed life in the Spirit was more in keeping with the Sermon on the Mount than with that of the spiritual and carnal Corinthians who were puffed up with their gifts of power and were judging others—even the great apostle Paul himself—by their use of those gifts (Matthew 5-7; 1 Corinthians 5ff).

John has another approach. In his writings he and Jesus bypass those gifts. It was given to Paul to expound these, especially in writing to the Corinthian church (1 Corinthians 12-14). *Jesus is completely vertical in John.* He receives everything from the Father. John keeps the spotlight on Jesus' Sonship all the time.

Sonship with the Father is the great demonstration and proof of His Messiahship, and Jesus is always insisting on it as the great proof in all those lengthy hassles He has with the Jewish leaders (see John 5-11). His Sonship is also the great proof for His being filled with the Spirit. At His baptism the Father's voice from heaven said, "You are My beloved Son; in You I am well pleased" (Luke 3:22).

What about Refillings?

Luke is especially inspired to write about

both the filling and subsequent refillings of the Holy Spirit in the Gospel of Luke as well as in Acts (see Luke 1-2, Acts 1ff). He shows clearly the distinction between the first filling and subsequent refillings. His point, and mine, is that the first filling (or infilling or enduement with "power from on high") was a distinctive and definite experience—not gradual, not a growth process. It was as definite an act as receiving a gift. Indeed, that is what it was, as Peter proclaimed on the day of Pentecost: "Repent, and let every one of you be baptized in the name of Jesus Christ for the remission of sins; and you shall receive the gift of the Holy Spirit" (Acts 2:38).

Later, after the infilling at Pentecost, they were "filled" again: "And when they had prayed, the place where they were assembled together was shaken; and they were all filled with the Holy Spirit, and they spoke the word of God with boldness" (4:31).

Jesus said, "Take heed how you hear. For whoever has, to him more will be given; and whoever does not have, even what he seems to have will be taken from him" (Luke 8:18). Believers who have the Holy Spirit are subsequently filled with the Holy Spirit and then have further refillings for new occasions. In

Acts, they are also known as people "full" of the Holy Spirit: "Seek out from among you seven men of good reputation, full of the Holy Spirit and wisdom, whom we may appoint over this business" (Acts 6:3). Philip the evangelist was one of them, and so was Stephen, who became the first martyr of the new Church.

After Pentecost the Spirit-filled life became the standard for every church and for every Christian. And in each case, whether for each congregation corporately or for each member personally, any subsequent "filling" was sudden—a fresh enduement of the Person and Power of the Holy Spirit (1:8).

4

Which Expression Shall We Use?

The major terms used to describe this experience are baptism, filling, infilling, power, enduement, sanctification, anointing. This does not mean that they all have the same meaning, but it means that in some way they describe what happens when we are filled with the Spirit.

The words *filling, infilling, fullness* are used mostly and seem to be agreeable to all schools of thought, especially if they are concerned about keeping "the unity of the Spirit in the bond of peace" (Ephesians 4:3). In other words, they do not want to be divisive, dividing Christians from Christians.

Ephesians 5:18 says, "And do not be drunk

with wine, in which is dissipation; but be filled with the Spirit." It is a command. We *must* be filled! However, Ephesians 5:18 does not refer to the *initial* infilling, but commands us to "keep on being filled" (literal). It implies that a first filling has already taken place.

There are those who say that "be filled" does not say all that happened at and after Pentecost. At Pentecost the Church was both "filled" *and* "baptized" with the Spirit (Acts 2). They tell us that not a few were "filled" with the Spirit *before* Pentecost (like Mary the mother of Jesus; Zacharias and Elizabeth, the parents of John the Baptist; also godly old Simeon and Anna and John the Baptist, who was filled with the Spirit even before he was born), but that at Pentecost they were "baptized" with the Spirit and also filled in a new way (see Luke 1-2 and Acts 1-2).

Sanctification

Sanctification is the word many use to describe this experience, especially the Wesleyan and "holiness" groups. They too have a record of mighty revivals. Thousands have crowded the altars of the great holiness camp meetings as well as other meetings, seeking to be sanctified. They also called it the "second blessing," equating it with "the filling."

Enduement with power

"Enduement with power" is another way to describe being filled with the Spirit. Jesus spoke of this when He told the disciples what would happen "not many days hence" at Pentecost, just as He was about to ascend to heaven: "But you shall receive power when the Holy Spirit has come upon you; and you shall be witnesses to Me in Jerusalem, and in all Judea and Samaria, and to the end of the earth" (Acts 1:8). This is what happened at Pentecost. And, indeed, it is the key verse to all of the great book of Acts.

The anointing

"The anointing" has become a popular expression for this experience.

It certainly was true of Jesus Himself, who was the Messiah, the "anointed one." He referred it to Himself in the first sermon He preached in His hometown synagogue at Nazareth. He began at Isaiah 61:1-2:

> "The Spirit of the LORD is upon Me,
> Because the He has *anointed Me*
> To preach the gospel to the poor;
> He has sent me to heal the
>   brokenhearted,
> To proclaim liberty to the captives

And recovery of sight to the blind,
To set at liberty those who are
      oppressed;
To proclaim the acceptable year of
      the Lord." (emphasis added)

Then He closed the book, and gave it
back to the attendant and sat down.
And the eyes of all who were in the
synagogue were fixed on Him.
    And He began to say to them, "To-
day this Scripture is fulfilled in your
hearing." (Luke 4:18-21)

I am always much moved by this Scripture
because it was also the text for the first sermon
I preached. It was in a rather large Lutheran
church in Hobart, Indiana, on a hot Sunday
morning in July. I was still a student at seminary, having finished my first year. My homi-
letics professor urged me to preach that
sermon. So, as was our custom then, I memorized it—every word of it.

The pulpit in that church was high and
beautiful like in a cathedral. Some steps from
the inner sacristy led to the door which I had
to open to get to it. I noticed there was a window near the pulpit—open.

I had no sooner started to preach when a sudden gust of wind came through that window, blew the door open behind me and at the same time blew my little sermon outline from my Bible in front of me. I can still see it slowly fluttering to the floor with all eyes on it. Our people would sit on edge and almost hold their breath when a student would preach— especially his first sermon: *What if he gets stuck?*

I *was* stuck. My memory went blank. Did I pray? Yes—right in the pulpit, not out loud but most earnestly. The answer came suddenly. Outwardly poised but inwardly turbulent, I turned around, closed the pulpit door, turned again to the congregation and started to speak. I can't recall what I said. I do recall that the Holy Spirit took the message I had memorized and, as I sought to follow, led me through—or should I say, brought the whole sermon *through me* in a new, refreshing and enlivening manner. What an experience—doubly memorable since it was my very first preaching experience. The Lord saw my desperation and gave me an anointing—a foretaste of what I was to know more fully later.

After Pentecost, "anointing" was much used, and by the time John wrote his Gospel, it seems to have been even more commonly used.

For example, in Acts 4 the whole Jerusalem congregation made it central in one of the most powerful prayer meetings in the book, as they prayed in the name of Jesus, "Your holy Servant Jesus whom You *anointed*" (4:27, emphasis added). The whole place was shaken where they were assembled, and they were all *again filled* with the Holy Spirit as part of a whole series of some of the largest answers ever given to prayer (see 4:22).

Still later, Peter, preaching for the first time to Gentiles in the house of the Roman centurion Cornelius, referred again to Jesus' filling when he said, "how God *anointed* Jesus of Nazareth with the Holy Spirit and with power" (10:38, emphasis added).

Later still, the apostle Paul, writing to his Corinthian congregation, declares: "Now He who establishes us with you in Christ and has *anointed* us is God" (2 Corinthians 1:21, emphasis added).

In Old Testament days priests, kings and prophets were anointed with oil, sanctified and set apart for their ministries.

The writer to the Hebrews gives us this precious insight into Jesus: "You have loved righteousness and hated lawlessness; therefore God, Your God, has *anointed* You with the oil of gladness more than Your companions" (Hebrews 1:9, emphasis added).

In John's first epistle he shows that now he majored in using "the anointing." For he writes:

> You have an *anointing* from the Holy One, and you know all things. . . . But the *anointing which you have received* from Him abides in you, and you do not need that anyone teach you; but as the *same anointing* teaches you concerning all things, and is true, and is not a lie, and just as it has taught you, you will abide in Him. (1 John 2:20, 27, emphasis added)

"Baptism" or "Filling"?

Shall we call this experience "the baptism" or the "filling" of the Spirit?

John the Baptist called it "baptism" and so did Jesus. It is interesting to note that both were filled with the Spirit—John even before he was born, and Jesus above others, thirty years after He was born of the Spirit—yet neither referred to the coming Pentecost as "the filling."

But today the word "baptism" is controversial and can be divisive. Many Christians are cautious about using the term; they want to play it safe and are usually agreeable to call it both baptism and filling, implying that the two are more or less synonymous.

Certainly on the Day of Pentecost people were both baptized and filled with the Spirit. But that does not mean there is no distinction between the two (Acts 2:1-4).

How Can We Know the Difference?

It helps to know *when, where, how* and *by whom* the term "baptism" is used. The sequences and order of events are very important in Scripture. We must let Scripture speak for itself. It has its own way of speaking right out and doing so without breaking its own inner unity.

Recently I asked a pro golf instructor what he thought was the hardest thing to learn about the golf swing.

"Balance," he replied.

It is easy to become unbalanced and go to extremes in seeking to be filled with Him, especially when we get into gifts and demonstrations and manifestations. We must be cautious not to grieve the sensitive Holy Spirit with our actions.

It appears that on the Day of Pentecost the "baptism" was corporate, while the "filling" was both *corporate* and *individual* ("all," "each," 2:5). What is not clear is whether the *baptism* also was individual.

When Jesus had spoken of the baptism, it was to a body: the "you" was in the plural, meaning "you all." Likewise, when He spoke His last word on earth to them, it was: "You [plural, "you all"] shall receive power when the Holy Spirit has come upon you; and you shall be witnesses to Me in Jerusalem, and in all Judea and Samaria, and to the end of the earth" (1:8).

Whether we use "baptism" or "filling," we must not teach more than Scripture declares.

Only once after Pentecost, in Acts, is "baptism" used of the Holy Spirit. This is interesting because other expressions are used for the various Spirit-filled experiences. And if "baptism" were the key word or the watchword, one might well expect it to be used again and again.

Peter, the original preacher in Jerusalem on the Day of Pentecost, did not use it again, except some years later. It was in the house of Cornelius, the first time he preached to Gentiles. The Holy Spirit fell on them while he was preaching Christ, and they were all converted and filled with the Spirit. Both at the same time. It was also like Pentecost because they also spoke with tongues. "Then," he tells us, "I remembered the word of the Lord, how He said, 'John indeed baptized with water, but you [plural] shall be *baptized* with the Holy Spirit' " (11:16, emphasis added). It is interesting that here Peter recalled and used the very same words Jesus used in Acts 1, ten days before the mighty outpouring and baptism of the Spirit on the day of Pentecost (see 1:5).

Only once more do we hear the word "baptism" for the Holy Spirit in the New Testament, this time from the pen of Paul. Many believe that Paul also had Pentecost in mind as he wrote to his congregation in Corinth: "For by one Spirit we were *all baptized into one body*— whether Jews or Greeks, whether slaves or free" (1 Corinthians 12:13, emphasis added).

Whatever else is not fully clear here, it is very clear that this is a *corporate* baptism into one body—the Church.

Many say in this Scripture Paul does not use the word "baptize" in the same sense that John the Baptist and Jesus used it when referring it to Pentecost. On that day, they say, it was *Jesus* who baptized them with the Holy Spirit and with fire, while here Paul says it is the *Spirit* who baptizes all into Christ and His body, the Church. Here it refers to regeneration, and there it refers to a further enduement of power for witnessing for Christ.

Pentecost, many say, was the birthday of the New Testament Church. But Scripture does not say that. It says they were *baptized* in the Spirit on Pentecost.

It is easy to lose the balance of Scripture if we say what it doesn't say. In any case, the word "baptize" is not the unifying word.

It is interesting that John very early in his Gospel introduces John the Baptist, who says that Jesus will "baptize with the Holy Spirit" (see John 1:33). Yet John does not again use the expression, though he is a major leader both in telling us what the Spirit-filled life really is and how we can enter into it.

Some Who Used the Word "Baptism"

Many renowned leaders used the term "baptism" to describe how they were filled with the Spirit. Their testimonies have helped multitudes, and we should know their stories. Let's hear about a few of them. The fact that they were not Pentecostals or charismatics but rather were used to challenge and inspire them tells us something. It tells us even more when we learn how definite and fulfilling and glorious and uncompromising their testimonies were. And best of all, that they were not divisive but were used by God to keep and widen and deepen the *unity* of Christians everywhere.

Charles G. Finney

The story of Finney's life and powerful revivals still fascinates people in all lands. To want to learn about revivals and yet avoid Finney is like wanting to know about golf and avoiding Jack Nicklaus.

When Finney describes his experience, one wonders what else he could call it but a "baptism" in the Spirit. He tells how "waves and waves of liquid love" flooded his being so that he literally "bellowed forth the unutterable gushings of his heart." He says he didn't even know there was such a "baptism." His unique conversion to Christ took place earlier on the same day, so Finney never thought of his "baptism" and filling with the Spirit as anything but distinct and subsequent to conversion.

Immediately Finney led people to Christ,

and a revival started in the Presbyterian church that began to transform the town of Adams, New York. He at once gave up his law practice and became God's lawyer, pleading God's case as no other ever did. He started to kindle the fire of revival wherever he went—a record that has seldom been exceeded since the apostles. He has been called the "apostle of revivals." His "baptism" was indeed an experience of new and great "power from on high" (Luke 24:49). Finney used the term "baptism of the Spirit" for his own personal experience.

Dwight L. Moody

D.L. Moody's experience was something like Finney's. Finney was the outstanding evangelist of our country in the first part of the 1800s, and Moody dominated the latter part of that century. He was a Christian and already having a strong ministry in Chicago when two Free Methodist women who came to his meetings and sat together at the front as intercessors told him they were praying for him to be empowered and filled with the Holy Spirit. Moody reacted at first: "Why don't they pray for many to be converted to Christ?" With love and burdened in prayer, they repeated that they were praying that he would be empowered by the Spirit. Moody was a humble man and began to agree. Then he began to be very prayerful about it.

Walking along a street in downtown New York the answer came—the Holy Spirit moved mightily on him. He went into a friend's house nearby, experiencing what he (like Finney and others) called the "baptism" of the Holy Spirit. No one but Moody knows all that happened in his room in that house; but we all know that Moody was empowered and became one of the greatest evangelists the world has ever known.

Moody used the term "baptism" freely, and preached it. He led many (especially students) into it. He never compromised his message or made the way cheap and easy. He would illustrate it with an empty glass, which he would suddenly fill to overflowing. Then he invited those who wanted to be filled as he had been to meet him there early the next morning.

The word "baptism" was the expression of the time for this "deeper experience" in those days before Pentecostalism fully adopted it and dispensationalism as fully avoided it.

Reuben A. Torrey

Torrey's experience was very definite and distinctive, but different. What was the same, however, was the way Torrey also called, preached and taught the "baptism" of the Spirit. He taught the "way in" was by repentance, obedience and faith.

More than once Moody would urge Torrey to preach on "the baptism of the Holy Spirit." Torrey, Moody recognized, was much gifted for this, and he led many into it. It became a vital part of his ministry as evangelist, teacher and pastor.

The voltage varied

Space forbids my mentioning many others, but my point is this: Their lives were changed, and they were used to change others. They had new power. The voltage varied, but they all had new power from on high.

Now we are in a new day again. God is doing a new thing, but it is new only because it is so old that it is new. The more we near the end, the more we will get back to that which made the original Pentecost more full than anything under that name since. No one group has a corner or a patent on all that happened on the Day of Pentecost. It's high time we quit fighting one another, and *all of us get back to Pentecost—all the way back*. All the way back to the very first verse of that great chapter, which says in no uncertain terms that "when the Day of Pentecost had fully come, *they were all with one accord in one place*" (Acts 2:1, emphasis added).

And it will not do to say we need to be filled with the Spirit to make us one. That infant Church was united in the greatest possible unity on earth *before* they were "all filled with the Holy Spirit." That set the pattern for the twofold action I plead for in this book: 1) they were all filled, and 2) they all *kept* the "one accord" unity of the Spirit at the same time. They kept it because they had it before they were filled.

And they were all filled because they had the unity as one of the conditions for it. Yes, the *final* condition.

Nothing is more sorely needed in this charismatic hour—in this day and age of the Spirit. God hasten the day when the Day of Pentecost will "fully come" again (2:1). In that Day this word of Jesus will be fulfilled again: "By this all will know that you are My disciples, if you have love for one another" (John 13:35).

Part 2

*Receive
the Holy Spirit*

5

A New Testament Formula

This "formula" is what you have been waiting for. The various biblical approaches I have been giving are essential to what, for me, has been a fresh discovery.

I do not call this approach new. It is old. But, like much in Scripture, it is so old that it is new. It does not only take us back to the New Testament—it takes us *all the way back to the mouth of Jesus Himself.*

Of course I have been familiar with the words "receive the Holy Spirit." But I have discovered how the words carry through the New Testament from the time they were given.

These words of the Lord are like a golden thread which stitches its way into and through the fabric of the New Testament. They become a watchword—*before* Pentecost and *at* Pentecost and *after* Pentecost—guiding into the Spirit-filled life and then guarding it.

This phrase is a unifying one. There are other expressions, but this is God's original word.

We have followed the course of these words through much of the New Testament. Now let's go the other way, all the way back to their source, the mouth of Jesus. From there it guides and guards the way into the Holy Spirit in fullest measure.

This formula is a phrase that, as I said, stitches through the fabric of the New Testament. We can actually see the seams. And the same seams help to keep the unity of Scripture, which is so paramount.

We can see how John, like a great football quarterback, calls the signals (which he got from the mouth of Jesus), both for receiving Christ and for receiving the Holy Spirit. John then keeps the ball in play and, unified with a team of New Testament leaders, advances the ball to the New Testament goal of the Spirit-filled life for every Christian and every church. It is a fresh approach to the dynamic and delicate field of the Holy Spirit!

John Tells It Like It Is

Only John takes us all the way back to these words of Jesus:

> Then, the same day at evening, being the first day of the week, when the doors were shut where the disciples were assembled, for fear of the Jews, Jesus came and stood in the midst, and said to them, "Peace be with you." When He had said this, He showed them His hands and His side. Then the disciples were glad when they saw the Lord. So Jesus said to them again, "Peace to you! As the Father has sent Me, I also send you." And when He had said this, He breathed on them, and said to them, *"Receive the Holy Spirit.* If you forgive the sins of any, they are forgiven them; if you retain the sins of any, they are retained." (John 20:19-23, emphasis added)

When John tells us what the other Gospel writers do not, it usually is something of utmost importance. So here, when Jesus "breathed on them," it was not just a little puff of air. Something profound took place, something life-changing. Not something merely symbolic and not just a foretaste of Pentecost, but a *real impartation of the Holy Spirit*.

A Great Inbreathing

Let me elaborate on this great inbreathing.

John's Gospel is full of buildups, and it is interesting to see how this inbreathing climaxes what the Lord promised concerning the Holy Spirit (chapters 7, 14-16).

Jesus did more than breathe *on* them: He breathed *into* them. This recalled His breathing "into Adam" (see Genesis 2:7). (The Septuagint, the Greek translation of the Old Testament, uses the same word in Genesis as Jesus uses here in John 20.)

Some say the Holy Spirit was not given until the Day of Pentecost. According to John, this is not true. The Holy Spirit actually was given—imparted, received—into the disciples, and imparted for the strong commission given with it: for binding and loosing, for forgiving and retaining sins and for their being sent forth in ministry as the Father had sent Christ. This new commission became their new mission, and it was not repeated. This can be done only through the indwelling Spirit.

Pentecost, according to leading commentators, came as a further enduement or manifestation of the Spirit whom they had already received. They received Him so definitely that they could pray as a body—a real *koinonia*—for ten days in the strongest kind of praying they (about 120 disciples together) had ever yet prayed: "in prayer and supplication" and "with one accord" in the famous upper room (Acts 1:14-15).

Some thoughts on this "receiving"

H.B. Swete writes that the Spirit "had been in possession of the Church from the moment that the risen Lord breathed into her the Breath of Life, although before Pentecost she was scarcely conscious of her new powers, and even after Pentecost realized them only by degrees."[1]

Bishop Westcott, in his commentary on John, is even stronger. He writes that this great new inbreathing of the Spirit expressed "the communication of the new Life or re-created humanity. . . . The act was not repeated. . . . It was 'once for all' . . . to the abiding body."

"The Gift of the Spirit," he continues, "finds

its application in the communication or with-holding of the powers of the new Life."[2]

Lenski, in his commentary on John, writes, "in the act of breathing by Jesus, whatever may be considered a symbol becomes at the same time an actual means of bestowal . . . accords with the purpose for which it is used."[3]

Then Lenski sharpens the point: "Let us understand once for all that any and every reception of the Spirit means the Spirit Himself, the entire and undivided Third Person of the Trinity, is received. . . . We can no more split up the Spirit than we split up the Father or the Son."[4]

In summary: He will now send His followers "as the Father has sent Me." He was sent *filled* and *full* of the Holy Spirit (see Luke 4).

Words of Jesus Himself

When and where and why did Jesus first speak these words?

It was on the day of His resurrection (Easter) in the evening when His disciples were gathered together in Jerusalem in the upper room. Christ had been crucified two days before. So, being full of fear, the disciples made sure the doors were all shut. Then Jesus Himself suddenly appeared in their midst. John was there and tells us the full story. He also goes back of that some months and tells us another original story:

> On the last day, that great day of the feast, Jesus stood and cried out, saying, "If anyone thirsts, let him come to Me and drink. He who believes in Me, as the Scripture has said, out of his heart will flow rivers of living water." But this He spoke concerning the Spirit, *whom those believing in Him would receive*; for the Holy Spirit was not yet given, because Jesus was not yet glorified. (John 7:37-39, emphasis added)

We must remember that John wrote this years later—many years later, as much as two generations. This tells us how alive these words of Jesus still were. It indicates not only how they came into being, but how consistently they must have been used.

John was a prime leader in using this phrase and in the ministry of getting people filled with the Spirit.

Peter at Pentecost

It is wonderful to see how the New Testament

leaders all agree on the use of this original phrase from the lips of Jesus. It also becomes their *method* for leading converts, and even entire congregations, into the full life of the Spirit.

All of this together makes for a profound ongoing unity. It continues to uphold the high Spirit-filled standard of New Testament Christianity and gives us a good insight into the way Scripture works hard to keep "the unity of the Spirit in the bond of peace" (Ephesians 4:3).

See how Peter preaches this on the day of Pentecost. Thousands of Jews were convicted of sin and cried out, "What shall we do?"

Peter answered, "Repent, and let every one of you be baptized in the name of Jesus Christ for the remission of sins; and you shall *receive the gift of the Holy Spirit*" (Acts 2:38, emphasis added).

It is distinct from salvation, but he wasted no time getting it into his message at once. With a fired-up, Spirit-filled congregation demonstrating this and supporting him, it was easy for Peter to give them both barrels right away: Get them converted to Christ and filled with the Spirit in the same meeting. It is not usually done, but in that kind of atmosphere it has often been done.

So now the 3,120-member Jerusalem church

continues in its original oneness and continues to keep on the high and holy standard of the fullness of the Holy Spirit and the fullness of Christ. Their "one accord" secret does not diminish; it only increases.

Peter and John

Peter and John teamed up after Christ's resurrection, and after Pentecost they continued as prayer partners. They went to pray one day in the temple but they never got to pray there, because right there by the gate called Beautiful, as they were about to enter the temple, sat a cripple begging for alms. All three were very prayerful, fastening their eyes on each other.

Peter and John prayed for him in the name of Jesus, and he was instantly healed and converted to Christ. Walking and leaping and praising God, he at once joined them as a witness when Peter preached to a new crowd that had gathered. The Holy Spirit continued to orchestrate the revival in the Jerusalem church. This all happened because of the power of the Spirit not only in Peter and John, but in the praying Spirit-filled congregation (see Acts 3-4).

In Acts 8 Peter and John teamed up again in another way in Samaria. A great awakening took place under the preaching of Philip the evangelist. There was great joy in the whole city, for many were healed and delivered from demons and converted to Christ. But they were not yet filled with the Spirit. This seems to have been a major part of John's ministry as well as Peter's. In any case the apostles at Jerusalem "sent Peter and John to them, who, when they had come down, prayed for them that they might *receive the Holy Spirit.*" They were baptized already (in the name of Jesus) and were Christians. But "then they laid hands on them, and they *received the Holy Spirit*" (Acts 8:14ff., emphasis added).

Notice the language. They did not pray for a filling or a baptism of the Spirit or for any particular charismatic gift or manifestation. They received Him . . . the Person of the Holy Spirit. And then He manifested His power with manifestations. We are not told what. In Acts, when "tongues" were given, Luke usually states it. The fact that Luke does not mention tongues shows that he gives them the same rating as Paul who asks, "Do all speak with tongues?" It is always best to stay with the Word of God and to say what it says.

Individual ministries

John, I linger to say, appears through his years

to continue to have the same ministry, not only of Christ, but of the Holy Spirit—the ministry which he later wrote about when he wrote his Gospel. His Gospel reveals the *source* and the Acts reveals the *course* of the Spirit's fullness.

A few years later Peter again used the same expression. The Spirit was poured out once again, this time for the first time among the Gentiles. For the first time in his life, Peter preached to them. It was in the house of a God-fearing Roman centurion whose name was Cornelius.

In those days the Jew-Gentile wall of separatism was very great, even more "separatist" than our separatist movements today. It could create a fight at the drop of a hat: Jews and Gentiles simply did not mix in worship.

The Holy Spirit gave Peter a fresh and different experience (manifestation) to make him willing even to go there. What a story this is in Acts 10!

Luke, in Acts, devotes two large chapters to this most eventful and miraculous story. So many things came together. Peter himself tells the story, and when he does he uses a number of expressions to describe what happened. He tells it this way:

And as I began to speak, the *Holy*

Spirit fell upon them, as upon us at the beginning. Then I remembered the word of the Lord, how He said, "John indeed baptized with water, but you shall be *baptized with the Holy Spirit.*" If therefore *God gave them the same gift* as He gave us when we believed on the Lord Jesus Christ, who was I that I could withstand God? . . . Then God has also granted to the Gentiles *repentance to life.* (Acts 11:15-18, emphasis added)

But when in the previous chapter he tells how he got those Gentiles "in," he uses the original well-tested expression, the same as he used before and which both he and John used when they teamed up in prayer for Samaritan believers to be filled with the Spirit: "Receive the Holy Spirit."

These are Peter's words: "Can anyone forbid water, that these should not be baptized who *have received the Holy Spirit* just as we have?" (10:47, emphasis added).

Dr. G. Campbell Morgan said Acts is the story of the glorious regularity of the irregular.

So here the Lord brought it all together differently, and in the same downpour of the

Spirit (repentance, new life in Christ, gift and gifts of the Spirit, baptism of the Spirit, water baptism).

But I also notice that this is the only time the term "baptism" is used of the Holy Spirit after Pentecost. In Acts Peter remembered verbatim how the Lord Himself used it before Pentecost. (Compare Acts 11:16 with Acts 1:5.)

Everything that happened in Cornelius' house seems to remind Peter of what happened a few years ago at Pentecost. All this is as instructive as it is exciting.

Paul Also Uses the Original Language

We've been waiting to hear from the great apostle Paul. Now comes his turn to go to bat on the subject. He was the founding father of many of the New Testament churches and kept them all on the original standard of being Spirit-filled. And he wrote letters to many of them to hold them to that standard, just as John and Peter and the other New Testament writers did.

It is interesting to see that these three weigh in about the same on the New Testament scale. And they use much the same language in getting their Christians and churches on that high level.

So, about twelve years after Peter's tremendous experience in the house of Cornelius (and time and sequences are important in Scripture) Paul uses the same expression *"receive the Holy Spirit."* He comes to the great city of Ephesus and finds about a dozen disciples of John the Baptist.

Here's how Luke tells it:

> And it happened, while Apollos was at Corinth, that Paul, having passed through the upper regions, came to Ephesus. And finding some disciples he said to them, *"Did you receive the Holy Spirit when you believed?"* So they said to him, "We have not so much as heard whether there is a Holy Spirit." And he said to them, "Into what then were you baptized?" So they said, "Into John's baptism." Then Paul said, "John indeed baptized with baptism of repentance, saying to the people that they should believe on Him who would come after him, that is, on Christ Jesus." When they heard this, they were baptized in the name of the Lord Jesus. And when Paul had laid hands

on them, the Holy Spirit came upon them, and they spoke with tongues and prophesied. Now the men were about twelve in all. (Acts 19:1-7, emphasis added)

Here is another case of the glorious regularity of the irregular.

They repented and were baptized under John the Baptist. Then they were baptized again in the name of Christ Jesus. Now, for sure they were Christians; and still Paul followed up on his original question—in this case by the laying on of his hands they *received the Holy Spirit* and were filled. It was clearly a definite "sudden, subsequent-to-conversion" experience, as the Spirit at once manifested His power with accompanying gifts of tongues and prophesy, just as Paul later taught: "as He wills" (see 1 Corinthians 12).

This is the way the mighty church of Ephesus started. It grew and grew and grew, awakening the whole city in one of the greatest awakenings of the whole New Testament.

Later in his life, not many years before his end, Paul again gives us some clear words when he writes to the Galatian churches.

He had got them into the Spirit-filled life and

on the Spirit-filled standard, and now he held them to it when they were in danger of losing it by wanting to add the law to it. They were flirting with legalism, a return to works, to what Paul calls "the weak and beggarly elements" (Galatians 4:9).

They thought they were adding to their spiritual life with the law, but in fact they were losing it. Paul was deeply disturbed and writes some of his sharpest words to the Galatians:

> O foolish Galatians! Who has bewitched you that you should not obey the truth, before whose eyes Jesus Christ was clearly portrayed among you as crucified? This only I want to learn from you: *did you receive the Spirit* by the works of the law, or by the hearing of faith? Are you so foolish? Having begun in the Spirit, are you now being made perfect by the flesh? Have you suffered so many things in vain—if indeed it was in vain? Therefore He who supplies the Spirit to you and works miracles among you—does He do it by the works of the law, or by the hearing of faith? (3:1-5, emphasis added)

A very unique verse: while holding the Galatians to their original high standard of the Holy Spirit, Paul tells us how they entered into that fullness. It was "by the hearing of *faith*."

And he uses the same tried, tested and true expression: "Did you *receive the Holy Spirit?*" He used the expression which Peter and John used. We can't improve on their message and method for getting people filled with the Spirit.

We remember that this expression came right from the mouth of the Lord Himself. This is the Spirit-empowered and Spirit-empowering Word, and we must enlarge on it.

Peter, Paul and John in Agreement

Peter and Paul and John, as I mentioned, weigh in about the same on the charisma scale in the New Testament.

But have you noticed how, when they write their epistles later, they put their whole weight down on sanctification and holiness of life and not on their earlier experiences of power?

Early on, Peter's spiritual weight was very much up and down. In the Gospel he even walked on water with Jesus, the only man who ever did. But Peter also sank, and sank in a hurry, when he took his eyes off of Jesus.

Later, after preaching his first message at Pentecost as a Spirit-filled man, thousands came to Christ. And on one occasion, even his shadow healed people as they were lined up on the street in Jerusalem. These and many other scenes demonstrated the new *power* side of his full life in the Spirit.

But have you noticed how when he later wrote his two epistles he says nothing of that and does not even mention the great power side of his life and ministry? Now he puts his whole spiritually mature weight down on sanctification (see 1 and 2 Peter).

Paul's emphasis on gifts is much the same. One can't help noticing certain developments in his epistles. Of course, any changes do not mean he backslid from his power-packed experiences in the Acts when he planted those churches and even saw whole Roman cities shaken through the power of the Holy Spirit. We must remember that he was still living in the period of Acts when he wrote most of his epistles. So there was no power loss or shortage with Paul.

However, in his letters to some of those churches, his tone of voice and vocabulary are different. Like Peter, he puts his weight down on sanctification, love, unity. The voltage is still there, but it is spent largely on the ongoing lifestyle of Christians with one another in the churches—how to walk and talk and work in the Spirit. Especially how to pray.

He is heavy, as I say, on sanctification. And we have such thoroughgoing words as these: "Now may the God of peace Himself sanctify you completely; and may your whole spirit, soul, and body be preserved blameless at the coming of our Lord Jesus Christ" (1 Thessalonians 5:23).

Paul in Ephesians

By the time he writes Ephesians (one of his latest letters), he is most comprehensive and fulsome and complete. The large picture is before him all the way through.

This comes to light best in his praying there. His prayer life is certainly at peak performance in Ephesians. It gives him away, as it does with all of us, because spiritually none of us is bigger than his prayer life. Paul was tall on his knees—so tall that he could reach heaven there. But nowhere is he taller than in his praying in Ephesians. The horizon keeps on widening with each great prayer:

. . . making mention of you in my
prayers: that the God of our Lord Je-

sus Christ, the Father of glory, may give to you the spirit of wisdom and revelation in the knowledge of Him, the eyes of your understanding being enlightened; that you may know what is the hope of His calling, what are the riches of the glory of His inheritance in the saints, and what is the exceeding greatness of His power toward us who believe, according to the working of His mighty power which He worked in Christ when He raised Him from the dead and seated Him at His right hand in the heavenly places, far above all principality and power and might and dominion, and every name that is named, not only in this age but also in that which is to come. And He put all things under His feet, and gave Him to be head over all things to the church, which is His body, the fullness of Him who fills all in all. (Ephesians 1:16-23)

Now he prays not so much for power to do great and mighty things, but for more revelation, for eyes to see what we have and to be what we are in Christ. He prays that we might be in line with the total body of the Church on earth, not just that of the local church or churches.

Full-capacity praying

For Paul, "Ephesians-praying" is full-capacity praying—the highest and most comprehensive prayer language. We should get on our knees with it and learn to talk this kind of language back to God. Paul's praying stretches his vocabulary to the limit in Ephesians.

The mighty Paul, filled to the full with the Holy Spirit as few ever have been, reaches to yet a higher level of fullness when he prays:

> I bow my knees to the Father of our Lord Jesus Christ, from whom the whole family in heaven and earth is named, that He would grant you, according to the riches of His glory, to be strengthened with might through His Spirit in the inner man, that Christ may dwell in your hearts through faith; that you, being rooted and grounded in love, may be able to comprehend with all the saints what is the width and length and depth and height—to know the love of Christ which passes knowledge; that

you may be *filled with all the fullness of God.* (3:14-19, emphasis added)

The Greek word for this total and complete fullness is *pleroma.* Here Paul is more than a Corinthian charismatic; he is a "pleromatic," praying to be filled with and unto *all* the fullness of God.

In Ephesians Paul reaches the totality of his prayer life. Praying "in the heavenlies" as from his spiritual Mt. Everest, he sees the complete picture: the complete Church of all saints; the complete comprehension of the Christian life related to the complete cosmos and to the complete family of God, urging us all to be sure to put on the complete armor of God for complete victorious praying.

In Ephesians he finally puts his whole weight down on Christian unity: we are to endeavor to "keep the unity of the Spirit in the bond of peace." And immediately he lines up the various unities which make up that great *oneness* in Christ (see 4:3).

All this and more is to take place in us when we are filled with the Holy Spirit.

No wonder he tells us one more time, and for the last time: "Be [being constantly] filled with the Spirit" (5:18).

All this without a trace of sectarianism or divisiveness.

Have you read Ephesians? I mean *really* read what's there?

After soaking up on Ephesians, my prayer is, "Lord, make me a pleromatic Christian . . . make me an Ephesian Christian!"

Endnotes

[1] Henry Barclay Swete, *The Holy Spirit in the New Testament* (Grand Rapids, MI: Baker Book House, 1976), 168.

[2] B.F. Westcott, *The Gospel According to St. John* (London: John Murray, 1924), 294.

[3] R.C.H. Lenski, *St. John's Gospel* (Minneapolis, MN: Augsburg, 1961), 1371.

[4] Ibid., 1373.

6

The Big Picture

*O*f we did not have John's Gospel we would not have either the last or the first word of Christ concerning the Holy Spirit. To him it was given to write the last revelation in the New Testament—not only in the book of the Revelation, but in his Gospel and epistles.

If we did not have John we could think of gifts (like those of First Corinthians 12) as being our "utmost for His highest." Let's make no mistake about it: they were great gifts then, and they are great gifts now. John himself had them, and they were active in his churches.

But John lived through it all. In the last analysis, when it comes to the Spirit-filled life and how to get into it, John gives us the tried and true way—the way he practiced and proved in his own life and in his long ministry, *just as He got it from the mouth of Jesus.*

With John the proof of the Spirit-filled life—and how it differs from our conversion to Christ—is more like this:

- From having a *"spring* of living water" in us, we now have *"rivers* of living water" flowing from our innermost being.

- Rather than stressing the new enduement of power, John stresses the *inward* working of the Holy Spirit.

- From having life in Christ, we move into *abiding and abundant* life in Christ.

- We get into full union and communion with Christ and a new and full prayer life, praying *in His name* as we see them doing in a new and Spirit-filled way after Pentecost.

- But the most significant difference is that now we learn the full *sonship* life . . . as it was with Jesus Himself, our real Example. We get everything from the Father and in answer to prayer; we are no longer our own or "on our own." But under His full ownership and care and direction and provision and guidance and—you name it. Gifts? Yes, to be sure, but "as He wills."

What a grand and glorious sequence unfolds in our Christian life:

1. The Holy Spirit gives us Christ (new birth);
2. Christ gives us the Holy Spirit in full measure;
3. The Holy Spirit, in turn, fills us with Christ to the full.

What a life! Who wouldn't want that?

And it becomes an unending pattern of "living it up" to the full, *even on earth.* Heaven will be glorious, to be sure. But we don't have to wait and die and go to heaven for this kind of a life. Jesus brought it all down here for us to experience and enjoy to the full right here and now.

At last we realize what life is all about. Christ is complete. The Holy Spirit is full. And the Fatherhood of God is real. At last we realize what is first. And what we are here for.

Receive *the Holy Spirit*

Receive is the key word.

To acquire a gift we must receive it. The word "receive" is the all-important word. That is the word of the Lord to get us "in."

And we are not just waiting to receive some kind of experience—we are to receive the Person of the Holy Spirit.

If, as I wrote earlier, the phrase "Receive the Holy Spirit" threads through the New Testament, it is the word "receive" that threads the needle.

Actively passive or passively active?

Church people have often discussed whether faith is actively passive or passively active. Both are involved, but there comes a moment of release when both come together and complete the action. Any earlier passivity becomes very active—and actually *receives* and *takes*. They are two parts of one beautiful act.

The Lord activates both the giving and the receiving of His Spirit. The moment the Lord breathed His Spirit into them He also quickened their spirits to receive Him. If their praying and faith were rather passive before (knowing that the Lord had it to give, but leaving it all up to Him to do so), it now became active and they received the Gift.

To receive a gift, I have to take it. And that is the real meaning of the word. It means "take the Holy Spirit." Faith, if passive before, is mightily active now.

The sensitive way the Lord works on both ends is unique. He is the Alpha and Omega of living faith. He prepares the praying person for His Gift. He leads him through testings and repentance and what we may call His "obedience school" into what Scripture calls the "obedience of faith." Then faith is alive and alert and well and very real. The receiving of the Holy Spirit is real—and not a mere "take it by faith" with nothing happening.

We receive the Holy Spirit in the same way we receive Christ as our Savior—as a Person. Not as an "it," not as an experience, but as a Person.

The Lord processes His gifts. They are free but never cheap. And the greater the gift the greater the process and the preparation of heart for it.

But at some point we must actively receive; we must *take* the Gift. Some people pray and pray for the Holy Spirit passively when all the while the Lord is ready, more willing to give than we are to receive His Gift, and bids us to take the Gift (the Person). And thank Him.

John said, "A man can receive nothing unless it has been given to him from heaven" (John 3:27). That is exactly the way Jesus offers to give us the Holy Spirit. And His Word about it is so plain: "If you then, being evil, know how to give good gifts to your children, how much more will your heavenly Father [or, "your Father out of heaven"] give the Holy Spirit to those who ask Him!" (Luke 11:13).

But we must ask in *faith*. Listen to James, the Lord's half brother, "Let him ask in *faith*, with no doubting, for he who doubts is like a wave of the sea driven and tossed by the wind. For let not that man suppose he shall receive *anything* from the Lord" (James 1:6-7, emphasis added).

Taking the Spirit

I repeat: we must at some point actually *receive, take* the Holy Spirit.

In a timely moment I once met a man who knew and spoke Greek. I asked him about the word "receive" used in this Scripture, and at once he said, "It means *take*."

Commentators say the same thing. H.B. Swete is very pointed: "The use of *labete* rather than *dechesthe* implies that the gift is not *opus operatum* [automatic], but a vital force which *must be met by personal effort, and not passively received*."[1]

Lenski is just as strong: "The aorist *labete* is decidedly punctiliar and denotes reception then and there, and not a process of reception that is to go on and on."[2]

Westcott, in his commentary on John, writes, "Receive, literally, *take*"[3] (John 20:22).

Other commentators agree: the receiving was an active and actual taking.

This is the "getting-us-in" word. It carries a lot of the burden of this book, because the big question is *How can I be filled with the Holy Spirit?*

Same Word "Receive" for Two Distinct Experiences

It is interesting and very instructive to see how John uses the same word and the same method for two different and distinct experiences.

In each case the word is "receive," and it is not some kind of glorious experience we are to receive, but it is a divine Person. And it is to take place on a very person-to-Person basis.

John wastes no time to get to this. Our first need is to become Christians, and John at once tells us how: "As many as received *Him*, to them He gave the power [right, authority] to become the sons of God" (see John 1:12). We "must be born again" Jesus declares in John 3. John does not wait to give us the clear answer, the how. (It was his own way as evangelist for many years.) Millions all over the world find Christ this way. Those who do this are "born again."

We no longer preach and teach that people should "receive salvation"—we ask them to receive Christ, the Person of Christ. And then we have salvation, and indeed, we have eternal life. Do not first seek some experience, but first receive *Him,* and He gives the assurance and experience.

The same is the method of John in the later portion of his Gospel, when he focuses on the Lord's disciples and their getting into and living the "deeper life"—the life of fullness in the Holy Spirit.

The same word is "receive" and this time it is "Receive the Holy Spirit"—a very different and distinct experience from their receiving Christ in the first chapter (20:22).

We are not, for example, urged in Scripture to receive "the baptism" or "the experience of sanctification" or "the filling" or "the power"; we are to receive the *Person* of the Holy Spirit. He then empowers, sanctifies, fills, gives gifts and graces and does all kinds of new things sovereignly, "as He wills." Instead of seeking experiences, we receive Him.

But an important point I want to make here

is that just as we have been following John's Gospel to help people to find Christ, we should do likewise in following and using his Gospel to help people who have found Christ to find and receive the Holy Spirit.

In brief, John seems to be saying, "In the early part of my Gospel I told you how to receive *Christ,* and now in the later part I told you how to receive the *Holy Spirit.* He too is a Person to be received definitely, as you did when you received Christ and became a Christian.

John's message and method, which He got directly from Jesus Himself, helped to bring about a unified Christianity in that day. *And it is just as greatly needed today.*

It will help us do the same two things so needed again: 1) lead people to be filled with the Holy Spirit, and at the same time 2) "endeavor to keep the *unity* of the Spirit in the bond of peace" (see Ephesians 4:3).

Let's Not Sectarianize the Holy Spirit

Pentecost was not meant to be divisive. Rather, the Holy Spirit came to an already perfectly unified Church and intensified that loving oneness while filling and empowering it for worldwide witnessing. And the book of

Acts reveals that no matter what happened through or to that Church, it kept the original oneness.

They even had it for ten days before Pentecost. Where? And how? When they were all praying together in the upper room "with . . . prayer and supplication" and when they were *all . . . with one accord*" (1:14, emphasis added).

Satan loves to divide and conquer. God loves to unite and conquer. He did so at Pentecost and after.

It's a sad day when so much divisiveness and splitting goes on among those who claim the high testimony of being filled with the Holy Spirit. This grieves the very Spirit they claim to be honoring: The biblical way is to preach and teach the Holy Spirit fullness without sectarianizing Him or His Church.

God give us all great grace here!

Spirit-filled Life Is Normal

The Spirit-filled life is not something strange in the New Testament. Nor is it something special. It is standard New Testament Christianity for every Christian and for every church.

Vance Havner had a way of saying we are so subnormal that if we got back to the New Testament normal we would be considered abnormal. We are settling for a lower level than the normal.

We shouldn't even settle for a revival. We do need it desperately, but not for the sake of having some kind of a revival. Even revival is not necessarily the normal, unless it gets us into the normal ongoing, prayerful, Spirit-filled Christian life. Just to be a booster rocket is not enough unless it gets the church into the orbit of a habitually holy life, as we see in the Acts.

In the Acts the plan is not for some kind of a revival in the Church; it is to get the whole Church filled with the Holy Spirit, and for it to continue and abound in the full life of Christ and of His Spirit as the normal, where it is normal for the Lord to add to it all the time those who are being saved (see Acts 1-6).

John the Baptist was Spirit-filled even before he was born. Jesus was filled with the Spirit even above others and above measure. At Pentecost the entire congregation was filled with the Spirit (corporately and individually). All the churches planted by the apostles were filled with the Spirit. From Pentecost to Patmos we meet Spirit-filled churches.

And finally, after a couple of generations, when many of the churches were leaving their "first love" and "first works," the Lord with a trumpet blast is calling them back to that normal first level—back to repentance and with the earnest words repeated seven times (something unheard of even in the New Testament): "He who has an ear, let him hear what the *Spirit* says to the churches" (Revelation 2-3, emphasis added). The churches were fallen from the high level of the *Holy Spirit*. And we see what that level is in their beginnings in the book of Acts.

If churches are now up and now down, in some kind of yo-yo revival experience, it is not normal, to say the least.

John in his Gospel is very helpful also here. He sets before us a normal, ongoing, abiding and abounding life in Christ as the standard and the norm. And he shows us the normal way they had in the New Testament for getting their Christians and their churches *into* it. We must make plenty of room for the Gospel of John and all it has to say to us—or even better, all that Christ has to say and wants to do in us.

My conviction is that we need John more than ever these days. I refer specifically to John 13-17; the chapters I'm calling on to carry a lot of the weight of this book.

Is the Holy Spirit Given for Sanctification or for Service?

He is for both, of course. After all, He is the *Holy* Spirit. And He is also *one* in all His manifold operations, which is equally important. He does not violate His own grand unity and oneness. No matter what all He does, He is one Person.

But there is more than one way *we* can sin against Him. He can be resisted, grieved, quenched, lied to, slandered and even blasphemed. These are the most sensitive sins in Scripture, because He is the most sensitive Person in the cosmos.

The area of His holiness is where we must watch the most, and we can let our emotions carry us out of biblical bounds very quickly here if we do not watch and pray and obey. This is where many of the specially gifted are much concerned today—which is good. And overdue.

Pentecost was as explosive as any experience, yet His unity and His holiness were kept together as one indivisible flame.

The same was true of His power for service and His sanctification and purity of life. In fact, at Pentecost the entire assembly of about 120 members had oneness in prayer and repentance and cleansing and purity of heart *before* they were filled with the Spirit. And this was their ongoing lifestyle. So the church at Pentecost is our real model.

I don't really have to choose between power and sanctification of life when it comes to His fullness in my life: but I often say if I *had to choose* I would choose holiness. Why? For many reasons, but especially because without holiness no one shall see the Lord (see Hebrews 12:14). Nothing more beautifully balances the power of the Spirit than His sanctifying power. He is forever the Holy Spirit!

I remember that even Judas had power and did many miracles in his Galilean days, teamed up for the powerful evangelization of the nation. Yet he betrayed the Lord into death and committed suicide as a "son of perdition." Jesus said:

> Many will say to Me in that day, "Lord, Lord, have we not prophesied in Your name, cast out demons in Your name, and done many wonders in Your name?" And then I will declare to them, "I never knew you; depart from Me, you who practice lawlessness!" (Matthew 7:22-23)

Have you not noticed how in all the epistles of the New Testament the emphasis is on purity and holiness of life—in a word, on sanctification? The apostle Paul makes clear that the *gifts* and operations of the Spirit are never meant to be manifested apart from the sanctifying *graces* [fruit] of the Spirit.

Paul, in fact, was adamant on this, and nowhere was he more eloquent about it at the same time, as we read in his famous love chapter:

> Though I speak with the tongues of men and of angels, but *have not love,* I have become sounding brass or a clanging cymbal. And though I have the gift of prophecy, and understand all mysteries and all knowledge, and though I have all faith, so that I could remove mountains, *but have not love, I am nothing.* (1 Corinthians 13:1-2, emphasis added)

This thirteenth chapter of First Corinthians is all about the superior gift of love, without which the gifts, however powerful, are as nothing. I'm not sure every Christian believes that—which is part of our problem.

I can see how John, the last New Testament voice, loved the word "anointing" for the Holy Spirit experience (see 1 John).

The oil in my car's engine must constantly lubricate the engine or there will be serious consequences. The oil and the gasoline are really the same petroleum functioning in two different ways. So the gifts and graces of the Holy Spirit are both operations of the one and same Holy Spirit.

And didn't I read of Jesus who, filled with the Spirit, "was *anointed with the oil of gladness* above His fellows" because He "loved righteousness and hated iniquity" (Hebrews 1:9, author paraphrase)?

John Clarifies Everything

John seems to have total recall when it comes to the Holy Spirit. Just as clearly as he recalls and retells the scenes which glorify Christ, he does the same when he relates the Person and work of the Holy Spirit.

While doing this, he clarifies both. For example, he certainly knows how to distinguish the way we are to receive Christ and become Christians from the way we are to receive the Holy Spirit and become Spirit-filled Christians.

Both experiences are real, distinct and distinctly different in John's Gospel. Which points out the fact that being filled with the Spirit is a distinct and distinctly different experience from regeneration (John 1:12-13; 7:37-39; 20:19-23).

Even when they take place at the same time, as in the house of Cornelius, they are not the same thing. They are distinct (see Acts 10-11).

We just heard how the whole new work of the Spirit came with words and special breathing from His mouth on the evening of His resurrection. In John 7 John takes us all the way back to another "great day of the feast" (the Feast of Tabernacles) when all at once Jesus stood and cried out:

> "If anyone thirsts, let him come to Me and drink. He who believes in Me, as the Scripture has said, out of his heart [or "innermost being"] will flow rivers of living water." But this He spoke concerning the Spirit, whom those believing in Him would receive; for the Holy Spirit was not yet given, because Jesus was not yet glorified. (7:37-39)

What a scene! He was a living demonstration

of those words which flowed from His own innermost being like a river: It is another original in John when Jesus for the first time spoke
of the greater and deeper work of the Holy
Spirit. Jesus later enlarged on this in the upper
room on the eve of His crucifixion, and then
again on the evening of His resurrection (see
13-17; 20:19ff.).

John writes all this later in life with clear
memory, telling how they were fulfilled to the
letter by the Spirit—the same Spirit who filled
John, who wrote, "But the Helper, the Holy
Spirit, whom the Father will send in My name,
He will teach you all things, and bring to your
remembrance all things that I said to you"
(14:26).

Final Thoughts on John 20:19-23

Far too much rides on this great inbreathing
and these penetrating words of Jesus to let this
all pass for a mere token.

Do we even stop to consider all that Jesus
said here? The fact that it was all new both for
Him and new for them?

1. "As my Father has sent me, even so send I
   you." How was He sent? By the Father and
   by the Holy Spirit. We are to have the same

life, the same prayer life, the life of the fullness of the Spirit and the same sending.

2. We are to be in the ministry of *remitting* and *retaining* sins as Jesus did and in partnership with Him, and by the same full power of the Holy Spirit.

This new commission was to be their new mission. This is a lot more than just a token. These words were quick and powerful, the very quickening by the Spirit, who had just raised Him from the dead (Romans 8:11). After His resurrection, "the last Adam became a [quickening,] life-giving spirit" (1 Corinthians 15:45).

In these days, when the guilt of sin is not preached very much, it is easy to read right past these pointed words of Jesus and just leave them pretty much alone.

Martin Luther did not do that. He called this the "office of the keys" and got enormous mileage out of them in the Reformation. He said, " 'The office of the keys' is the peculiar church power which Christ has given to His Church on earth to forgive the sins of penitent sinners unto them and to retain the sins of the impenitent as long as they do not repent" (Luther's Catechism).

To fulfill these words of Jesus we must "receive the Holy Spirit" and be filled with Him. Only *He* can accomplish this work of God.

The Larger Picture

What more should I say about John which I have not already said?

He emerges as the final great charismatic/pleromatic apostle of the New Testament. Indeed, of the whole Bible. With him the truth about the Holy Spirit comes full circle and complete—like the rainbow around the throne of God.

At last it is shown how John emerges as the prime apostle—the first apostle in this highly sensitive field of the Holy Spirit. Filled with the Spirit at Pentecost, he had all the gifts and graces which He bestowed. He and Peter teamed together in prayer, and together in Samaria they prayed for many new believers to receive the Holy Spirit. All were filled and demonstrated their new powers (Acts 3 and 8).

In his later years he lived in far-off Ephesus where he headed the churches which Paul earlier planted and established as Spirit-filled churches (Revelation 1-3). John is the last and only apostle in Scripture with the gift of prophecy supreme, and wrote the last and greatest prophetic book of all—the book of the Revelation.

Though John had the gifts of the Holy Spirit in full measure, when he (also there in Ephesus) wrote his matchless Gospel he did not even mention the gifts which Paul enlarged on in First Corinthians 12-14. He did not even mention the gift of tongues, though he had that gift as fully as Paul or any other at Pentecost.

This does not mean that those gifts were no longer in use. On the contrary, they were functioning in a more complete and more fully regulated manner. In any case, they were not allowed to do other than "keep the unity of the Spirit in the bond of peace" (Ephesians 4:3).

John, as I have pointed out, does seem (at least in his late writings) to like the phrase "the anointing" of the Spirit (see 1 John). But when he comes to the creative words for "receiving the Holy Spirit" he puts his whole weight down on them. And he keeps his weight down on them and helps others to do the same. I would say that from the day John "weighs in" with those words, he keeps the same weight for two or three generations of glorious ministry.

When I read many books on a certain subject, they will certainly differ, but where they say the same thing, I really listen. It is most inviting to read how the New Testament leaders say the same thing about receiving the Holy Spirit. This is more than a coincidence—it is the Word of God.

Endnotes

[1] Henry Barclay Swete, *The Holy Spirit in the New Testament* (Grand Rapids, MI: Baker Book House, 1976), 166.

[2] R.C.H. Lenski, *St. John's Gospel* (Minneapolis, MN: Augsburg, 1961), 1372.

[3] B.F. Westcott, *The Gospel According to St. John* (London: John Murray, 1924), 294.

Part 3

Testimonies

7

Armin's Testimony

As I mentioned before, I spent seven months seeking to be filled with the Holy Spirit. I was already in the ministry and had seen wonderful results. I had even experienced my first revival.

Why so long? For one thing, I was yet unschooled and unskilled in much of Scripture. Yes, plain Scripture. I was continually asking the Lord, "Dear Lord, if You can show me more for my life and ministry from Scripture—plain Scripture and plenty of it—I want it."

The Lord did just that—quickly. And I must just as quickly say that all of my decisions for Christ since I have come to know Him have been made in the light of the Word of God where it is plain and plentiful. In the same breath let me say that it is amazing that we could ever miss on this! It certainly is wonderful that the great things of the Lord are found in the plainest of Scripture. So we are without excuse.

For me it is not enough to say I must know and be led by the Holy Spirit. I believe that with all my heart; but if I come across a "doctrine" that is not also according to the plain Word of God, it's not for me. It's that simple.

The Search

So I had to get information on the fullness and power of the Holy Spirit clearly from plain Scripture. That took time, because I did not know much about the Holy Spirit in this way. I did not mix around with those who professed to know. (We were very "separatist" in our denomination, but we were very strong for Scripture as the inspired Word of God.)

I began to meet some who claimed to be filled with the Spirit, and that quickened my pursuit. But I was also greatly disturbed, because some of those (and they were outstanding Christians) who claimed to be Spirit-filled fought others who made the same claim. I couldn't figure this out. But instead of letting it throw me, it made me search the more for answers.

As I began to search Scripture, the Lord began also to search me! I even dug into the Greek roots of words and, as I stated earlier, the Word dug into my roots—and they were not Greek! They went back, far back, to Adam . . . and anything called *sin*. All were under the search of Holy Scripture.

In our area there was almost a constant feud between those of "Pentecostal" and those of the "holiness" movements: between those who stressed the "power" aspect and those who stressed the "sanctification/holiness" aspect of the Spirit. This has changed now. But it was very real in the 1930s. I was stretched. But all this was good, I later found out. God was working me over!

It took some time. The price for the gift of the Spirit is the same for us as it was for those who received it in the New Testament. There are no bargains or get-rich-quick schemes with God.

The Twofold Christian Life

It did not take me long to see in Scripture that there is what we call a twofold Christian life: 1) that of becoming a *Christian* and 2) that of becoming a *Spirit-filled* Christian. The language for this varies, but the distinction or difference is clear.

It is not clear in many churches today. Many proclaim Christian truth and assume that their hearers are all Christians. They do not lead their people into personal faith in Christ and *assurance* of eternal life. This leads to presumption, false hope, false peace and false comfort. This is very serious. It is not the way of the Word of God.

The same thing is happening when it comes to the Spirit-filled message and life. The New Testament does not assume or presume here. It is as clear on our need for finding and living the Spirit-filled life in Christ as it is for finding Christ and knowing for sure that one is a Christian.

Though the "way in" to the Spirit-filled life is very plain, it took me a while and many experiences to find it. God had to work me over and simplify me. The Lord, I learned, does not dump the Spirit on an unprepared vessel.

Power and *Sanctification*

I wanted both the power and the sanctification that the opposing movements of the day taught. I saw right away that holiness is primary. Why? Simply because God is holy. The

Spirit is a *Holy* Spirit. "Without holiness no man shall see the Lord" (Hebrews 12:10, 14, author's paraphrase).

The "holiness" people also had other expressions, including "second blessing." The more I pursued with Scripture, the more I avoided any expression that would lead to sectarianism. But I did not avoid the idea that the Scripture pictures a blessing which is subsequent to conversion—subsequent even if it takes place at the same time. And certainly, distinct from conversion to Christ. But I never argued the point. And so I pursued.

I was greatly convicted of my need, both of power and of sanctification. In fact, at one time I thought of quitting the ministry because I saw that the Lord did not send His disciples out into further ministry—would not even let them go—until they were "endued with power from on high" (Luke 24:49). But quickly the Lord got to me with this word: "He gives the Holy Spirit to those who *obey Him*" (see Acts 5:32). That was a great help. So I pursued the way of obedience.

Hindsight is a great teacher. In my search, and in His searching me, I see that I got into some self-effort and legalism. I suppose it is difficult to avoid this if one is doing a lot of praying and self-examining. I was *active in prayer, but passive in faith.* I see it all clearly now. I prayed continually. Though I actively praised and worshiped the Lord in these longer seasons of waiting on Him, my *faith* was almost entirely passive—leaving it all up to God to "do it."

I was mixed up. I would leave the *manifestations*—the way He wanted to fill me—all up to God, but in reality I was seeking the manifestations themselves. *I did not know or discern the difference between seeking them (which in Scripture He never asked me to do) and actively accepting and receiving Him* (the Holy Spirit Himself, in person) and then letting Him manifest Himself "as He wills" (1 Corinthians 12). I was putting fillings and feelings ahead of faith, putting the cart before the horse. In this case the cart was full of fascination and even ecstatic feelings. But there was no horse!

Process of Elimination

It took me a while to find out the dangers of seeking manifestations. I well remember my hunger when I would read testimonies like Charles Finney's. When he described his baptism in such flood tide language ("waves and waves of liquid love flooded my being, so that I literally bellowed forth the unutterable gushings of my heart" . . . and even spoke of asking the Lord to stop or he would die), I quickly got down on my knees and prayed: "Lord, that's what I want!" But nothing happened. There were no waves. Not even a ripple!

Later I learned that the Scripture does not speak of hunger in that way; it speaks of hungering and thirsting after *righteousness*, and that such would be *filled* (Matthew 5:6).

I also read of D.L. Moody, who also received a mighty baptism of the Spirit. We know that after it he was different and became the greatest evangelist of his time, moving two continents closer to Christ and His cross. He freely called this experience his "baptism in the Holy Spirit." And, as I said before, he used it in his own preaching and leading people into what he also freely called the "filling" of the Holy Spirit.

All this stirred me deeply. And I again got down on my knees and prayed: "Lord, that's what I want." I was willing to call it the baptism or any other term in Scripture. But again, nothing happened! Nothing! Often I was discouraged and confused. I at times prayed with some who claimed high-powered experiences because they were considered strong and very reputable leaders (I sought only such for help) especially in the "holiness" and "Pentecostal" movements.

I kept on in God's Word and read the experiences I considered reliable—those who made their mark in the Christian life and ministry. I did not merely want to play it safe; I wanted no nonsense, no error, and wanted to give no room for the devil. For me it has to be biblical, a main thing and a plain thing. I needed to avoid going off into the deep end.

One important leader said, "If the devil can't hold you back, he will try to shove you into fanaticism and make you useless." Many voices had to be filtered through my mind. You may not have to go the way I did, but "God's way in" is what counts, and that is very much the same for us all.

When it came to tongues and more ecstatic experiences, I found myself proceeding by a process of elimination. For example, when some tried to manipulate me to get me to speak with tongues or to "praise Him faster; it will come," I learned more about praise and worship. I knew most of us were stingy with praise and worship, and I did learn a lot about *praise and worship praying*. Great! But I refused to race into something unreal or mechanical. And as for the Holy

Spirit falling on me and filling me (as some thought), nothing happened.

Mixing with all schools of thought in my search was good, because later I found out the Lord wanted to use me with any and every group and denomination. I wanted no sectarianism. I agree with D.L. Moody, who said if he thought he had any sectarian blood in him he would ask Him to drain it before nighttime!

Some "Iffy" Methods

One night when I attended an all-night prayer meeting in Brooklyn, the leading minister in charge came to me (I was kneeling with many others), laid hands on me and urged me to "just let yourself go" and even suggested that I let myself go blank. That alarmed me and very much surprised me that this man whom I held in high esteem would engage in that kind of a method.

I said nothing (out loud), but I said to myself: *That's wrong. I'll not do anything like that. God never says to do that in His Word; it is dangerous and even spiritualistic. It leaves room for a wrong spirit or spirits. It is not the way of the Holy Spirit.*

In any case, nothing happened.

I've seen the real gift of tongues, and it is

wonderful. But I've seen a lot that is not wonderful! It certainly is a field where Satan does a lot of counterfeiting. One does not have to go the dangerous and "iffy" way that pastor recommended to me.

There is a right way in Scripture, and it is wonderful. God is not the author of confusion. And we don't have to get into false experiences, and then later test them to find out if they are genuine. Of course, if you have had something like that, then by all means have it tested and proven according to Scripture. It is not within the compass of this book to get into all of that. But the Lord is loving, merciful, forgiving and answers prayer.

Biblically, and especially in the life of Christ Himself (who is not only our Savior, but our full Example and Role Model in this great matter of being filled with the Spirit), I saw there are two major conditions to being filled with the Spirit: *prayer* and *full obedience* (the "obedience of faith").

The way of faith is always the way of the Lord and of the Word, and it is always (there) a *living* faith, a God-given faith, not something worked up but given in answer to prayer. And there must be faith in our praying or it is not even Christian. James in his epistle sounds out strongly and clearly, "But let him ask in *faith*, with no doubting, for he who doubts is like a wave of the sea driven and tossed by the wind. For *let not that man suppose that he will receive* anything *from the Lord*" (James 1:6-7, emphasis added).

It took me seven months to go the whole round in my seeking. You do not have to do that.

There are seven questions, all very simple, which will help you or anyone who seeks to be filled with the Holy Spirit. They are neither emotional nor intellectual.

You don't have to work up your emotions, and you don't have to go to college to learn them (though many do, and the Lord meets and fills them there).

They are very plain and simple *conscience* questions, and they take us at once to the tap root and deepest depths of our being. They have everything to do with being filled with the Spirit of God who is *holy*.

These questions lead us along the pathway of "obedience of faith"—all the way "in."

Seven Simple Questions

1. **Am I** *truthful*? That is not an emotional question, nor is it a highly intellectual ques-

tion. But it has everything to do with being filled with the Spirit. Why? Because Jesus is the Truth, and the Holy Spirit is the Spirit of Truth. And anyone who is to be filled with the Spirit must be a very truthful person.

Are there any conditions under which I tell a lie? A little lie? *God cannot lie*, and He will not have us try to do it for Him. Satan is a liar and the father of lies. Any kind of lying or a lying spirit must be dealt with, confessed and repented of. Do I stretch the truth? Do I exaggerate? In court we are asked to "tell the truth, the whole truth and nothing but the truth." Jesus holds court in us (we are His courtroom), and that is exactly what He (our real Judge) asks of us in order to fill us with His Spirit— the Spirit of Truth.

2. Am I *honest*? That too is not an emotional or intellectual question. But it has everything to do with being filled with the Spirit. Jesus Himself asks it, and He went that way when He was filled (above measure, and above any others) with the Spirit: He "loved righteousness and hated lawlessness," therefore He was "anointed . . . with the oil of gladness above [His] companions" (Hebrews 1:9). When John the Baptist baptized Him in the river Jordan, He told John: "Thus it is fitting for us to fulfill all righteousness" (Matthew 3:15). The Holy Dove, the Holy Spirit descended on Jesus, and He was filled.

Jesus also taught that. It is His way for us too, for He taught, "Blessed are those who hunger and thirst for righteousness, for they shall be filled" (5:6).

Some want to be spiritual without being fully honest. When we ask, "Are you honest?" they just want to talk about something "spiritual." It doesn't work!

It really means, practically: Can I be trusted in money matters? (And we all know how much money matters!) Have I taken anything? Stolen anything? Scripture says, "Let him who stole steal no longer" (Ephesians 4:28). Yes, and let him also take back what he has stolen!

Many a revival "came through" just at this point of making restitution. I'm not talking about the money you borrowed on loan and have made proper agreement to pay. I'm talking about anything you've borrowed that you haven't given back. Or "forgot" to pay back! The devil whispered to you: "Forget it. . . . Nobody remembers it."

The old liar! At least three if not four parties know all about it: 1) the devil knows about it; 2) the Lord knows about it; 3) you know about it; and 4) the party you borrowed from and didn't pay back most likely remembers it! (People usually have long memories when it comes to money!)

I once heard a friend pray: "Lord, don't let me do anything I'll have to confess if a revival comes."

That says plenty. The filling of the Holy Spirit is revival . . . and then some! And to be filled we must face and confess and repent of anything in our life that is not 100 percent for the Lord.

The Holy Spirit breaks through

This calls to mind one of our church revivals where the Holy Spirit "broke through" in the congregation. One elder, a dear man, teaching the adult Sunday school class, and heavily involved in all the work of the church, had borrowed $1,000—$500 from an old preacher and $500 from another person so he could go to Florida and invest it in what he thought was a good real estate deal. He went there and lost it all! Some time later he returned, got busy in his church again, but "forgot" about the $1,000 he lost. He again resumed his leadership there and also taught Sunday school.

There was much prayer. I preached there for

many weeks. And we were expecting revival. But there was hindrance—a block. The atmosphere was negative with no "give" to it. We were earnestly asking the Lord to show us any hindrance, etc. Then I began to hear about this leading elder. People knew about his Florida venture but had not talked about it. I was really surprised, for he was a good man and a real leader.

It was a Saturday. I said to the pastor, "We must go to see him—today."

He was surprised to see us, and really surprised when I confronted him with the Florida "deal." I felt very tender because of the total picture of our many weeks of meetings there. He began to weep and said, "But I don't have the money!"

I replied, "Dear brother, it really does not depend on whether you have the money. If you would but take your weary legs to each of these two parties, ask for forgiveness and simply give each $5 every time you get a paycheck, in that way you would at least start to pay back the money. You are a leading elder in this church, and I believe this would help bring the revival."

He cried. The pastor and I cried.

"Pray for me," he said. "I'll have to face the whole congregation with this." Sunday came, and so did the revival! He sat just a few rows from the front with his wife, and suddenly, before I got to preach, he arose. Immediately we all sensed a divine "give" in the service and atmosphere. Tearfully he confessed his sin before the whole congregation and asked forgiveness as he led the way to the altar and continued his repentance before the Lord.

It was like pulling a plug, and the Holy Spirit began to flow! Others at once stood up, asking for forgiveness for things they had said and done. On and on it went, both at the altar and among people in the congregation. What a melting time, as the heavens opened up. The revival "broke through."

And we did not get out of the church until the afternoon.

Many things happened which I don't have room to tell here. But the point is that the Holy Spirit answered prayer, orchestrated the honesty and the repentance and did "His thing" in the church—brought His own revival.

If the Holy Spirit doesn't do it . . .

I have said it quite often recently: *If the Holy Spirit doesn't do it, there is nothing to it!*

In Canada, the Holy Spirit broke through

into revival in a college as I was preaching in special meetings dedicated to revival. The "break" came when students were broken, confessed their sins and "hit bottom" on repentance. Some had to make restitution, which was costly. One had to go back and face border customs and was not sure if he would get back. That was in God's hands.

Much prayer went up. The whole school became a school of prayer those days. Again, there is no space here to tell the many things that resulted. Many had to face their finances, pay their bills and even write home confessing certain sins and asking forgiveness. In some cases "the revival" not only came to their homes and families but also took hold in their home churches.

In another even larger school in Canada much of the same took place. In fact, it was an even greater revival. It went on and on through the whole school, night and day, and all classes were suspended for over three days. In different parts of the world I still meet those who were revived in that revival. Some were called into the ministry and some became missionaries.

Who can tell all the blessings and benefits of even one such revival? To God be all the glory!

3. Am I *prayerful?* We do not read that Jesus sought any particular kind of manifestation or experience. But He did seek. And He was very, very prayerful. That is primary: there is no record in Scripture, or anywhere else, of anyone who was filled with the Spirit who was not a very *prayerful* person. And there is no record of anyone *continuing* to live as a Spirit-filled person who does not *continue to be* a very prayerful person. So, whatever is the form of experience or manifestation, this is and continues to be the first condition for the Spirit-filled Christian life.

4. Am I *obedient?* And with this goes the second great condition—portrayed in the life of Christ—that of *righteousness* and complete *obedience* to the Lord and to His Word. When these conditions are met, Satan may try and test and hinder and do his thing, but He cannot get in.

God also confronted me about full obedience and honesty concerning my "money matters" when I sought to be filled with His Spirit. This included making any confession and restitution. I had to deal with it.

Years ago, I recalled—even before I knew I was a Christian—I had stolen some nickels and dimes from mother's purse. It was one of those little old black purses which snapped together, and I knew that my mother kept it in the kitchen cupboard.

Now I was even a minister! What made me very broken in my repentance was that my folks were rather poor and had to be very careful with even nickels and dimes. In those days, as a lad in Pennsylvania, I did more than one job for a nickel. The fact that I had *stolen*, and was a minister's son (Dad was a Lutheran minister with two country churches at the time, mostly farmers, and no one had much money then) really got to me! In the course of the years I had given my folks a lot more than those nickels and dimes, and I had let it go at that.

But no—the Holy Spirit was not satisfied with that. Now in my fresh and "deeper" heart searching He convicted me of this, and I knew I must confess it and make it right. So I wrote home, confessed it and sent a check for more than I thought I had stolen.

As in all such cases, it not only released me, but did something in our home.

The importance of conscience

Conscience is the taproot of our being. There is nothing deeper in man than conscience; and when we repent and get right with God and man at that level, it is real. There the Spirit flows, from our "innermost being." This is not emotionalism, and it is not intellectualism—it is *conscience* business with the living God and His Holy Spirit. Emotions and intellect alone do not bring the Spirit's quickening. They glow and flow in the Spirit, to be sure. But they do not "bring the Spirit."

Jesus also spoke out His own experience when He said: "Blessed are those who hunger and thirst *for righteousness*, for they *shall be filled*" (Matthew 5:6, emphasis added).

Someone said, "God will take care of our obedience to Him." Peter once said it this way: "He gives the Holy Spirit to those who obey him" (see Acts 5:32).

"Obedience is better than sacrifice" (1 Samuel 15:22, author's paraphrase). It will also purify and control our emotions. I notice how quiet an audience gets when I declare any "conscience truth." But consciences come alive with "conviction of sin."

Most leaders agree that the revival we really need will bring conviction of sin and repentance and get us into the depths of biblical holiness. Sanctification will not take the place of power but will make it truly biblical. After all, most of the epistles major in sanctification and holy living. They are more revivalistic with renewal truth than evangelistic.

5. **Am I *pure*?** This also is not an emotional or intellectual question. We all know (or should know) that it has everything to do with being filled with the Spirit who is *holy*. It is not down the line on the list—it is the bottom line!

Jesus said, "Blessed are the pure in heart, for they shall see God" (Matthew 5:8). When we heed it (not only hear it), the Holy Spirit makes it real. The fact is, the Sermon on the Mount in Matthew 5 is *now* truth, revival truth, Spirit-filled life and living truth. "Blessed *are*," Jesus keeps on saying here.

"Am I pure?" means in my relation with the opposite sex. And, in our day, it also means with my own sex.

If we are to be clean we must "come clean." Calvary precedes Pentecost, and cleansing precedes the filling of the Holy Spirit. He does not fill unclean vessels but cleanses them with His precious blood so He can fill them. And "if we confess our sins, He is faithful and just to forgive us our sins and to cleanse us from all unrighteousness" (1 John 1:9). It's not enough to say, "Lord, *forgive* me." We must also say,

"Lord, *cleanse* me." We do not pray for cleansing and then keep right on living in the same sin and uncleanliness—secret or otherwise. We are praying to be cleansed *from* all unrighteousness. We cannot do any of this. He alone can forgive, cleanse and fill us. He even initiates and inspires the whole process; and every desire for God comes from God.

God does not want to fill an *unclean* vessel. So He deals with us about those things, gets us to face them, repent of them and be cleansed of them by His precious blood (see 1 John 1:7, 9).

I knew my hunger and thirst to be right and to be "filled" came from the same Lord and Holy Spirit whose desire was to fill me. It was even more His will than it was mine. For, as Scripture says, it is He who "works in us both to will and to do after His own pleasure." And He is "more willing to give the Holy Spirit" to those who ask than a father is willing to give good gifts to His children. It is wonderful to know this. (See Philippians 2:13 and Luke 11:11-13.)

6. Am I *easily offended*? This shows up the *self* which must be dealt with. In fact, it has been dealt with. When Christ was crucified, that too was crucified with Him. Like every-

thing else in this process, the *Lord* must do it—has done it—will do it. But we must face it all and deal with it, seeking His face and believing Him to do it.

We go "from faith to faith" in the Christian life. But all this process can happen in a hurry. It need not take months, as in my case. But we must face the Lord fully and deal fully with Him about *everything* in our lives.

Real faith, real filling

Let me quickly insert here that by this process of obedience the Lord inspires and gives the faith we must have to receive the Gift of the Spirit Himself in Person. This is the "obedience of faith." The final step of receiving is then very real: real because the Holy Spirit is alive through the whole seeking process, readying and steadying and leading to the act of receiving Him personally.

This is the way of *real* faith and needs to be given as the answer to any who merely "take it by faith" and nothing happens. Which is not *real* faith. When we go God's way, something *really does happen: The infilling of the Spirit is real!*

So I must deal with the "finer points" like being easily offended—which highlights other sensitivities of the self-life—and also a critical spirit or a gossiping spirit. A "watch and pray" spirit must be set up instead. The Holy Spirit, using His Holy Word, will help us face and deal with a whole brood of wrong attitudes which are called sin, and which the Lord has dealt with in His death for us on the cross.

"Faith comes by hearing [heeding], and hearing by the word of God" (Romans 10:17). We learn through Him to "faith our way through" it all.

Let's make sure that we continually *search Scripture so they can search us* and lead us through in the right way—God's way.

7. *What am I living for?* This is really the big question. My dedication to God must be full and complete. The chief end of man, says a catechism, is to glorify God and to enjoy Him forever. We are here to live the Christ-life— the Christ-*filled* life—and to this end we must be filled with His Holy Spirit, even as *He Himself was filled to live that life.*

My Final Step Settled It All

Now I must tell you how it all finally happened.

I was preaching in a special evangelistic series in a Baptist church in New York City, not far from the Manhattan Bridge. It was arranged by the young people of that church, and many were praying for revival.

I had for months been prayerfully seeking to be filled with the Spirit. Since we had no Saturday night meetings I went to Brooklyn one Saturday to pray with another church group in an all-night prayer meeting, longing for God to "meet me."

My praise and worship was active; my faith was passive. Nothing happened.

Then came Sunday, the day I shall not forget. I preached but recall nothing of that. What I do recall is the prayer meeting we held *after* the evening service. It was a beautiful, rather new church, and we held that evening service in the lovely spacious basement auditorium.

I wanted to get the matter of the Holy Spirit settled in my own life and was so burdened about it that I had little desire to pray about anything else. So I withdrew a little from the others and quietly prayed the Lord to clear this all up for me and settle it.

With that I sensed the Lord Himself drawing near. And (also quietly but very clearly) He questioned me (no audible voice, and yet I knew it was He): "You are a Christian?"

"Yes, Lord."

"How did you get saved?"

"Lord, it was by faith. I had a struggle for years, like Luther. I tried everything."

"But it was by faith?"

"Yes, Lord."

"Now what is it you want?"

"Lord, I want to be filled with the Holy Spirit from the innermost to the uttermost."

"Is there any other way than by faith? Don't you know that 'without faith it is impossible to please Him'? (Hebrews 11:6 leaped into my mind.)"

I saw the whole thing at once, right there and then!

I saw that I had been seeking *manifestations* and *experiences*. Good ones, to be sure. Experiences like those I heard about and read about.

At once I prayed, "Lord, I'm done praying about this right now! Right now I *take the Holy Spirit to fill me from the innermost to the uttermost. And I don't care if I ever have a wave or a ripple. It's settled right now."*

It was near midnight. I excused myself and left the prayer meeting to walk to my room. I was not married then and was staying in a guest room on that floor near the front of the building.

Suddenly, as I was leaving the prayer room, I

began to feel as if I was wrapped in a cloud of glory! It was a manifestation of the Spirit. And I had never read about one like this in Finney's or Moody's or anyone else's experience. It was His manifest Presence, right there as I walked on into my room.

Then when I got to my room and soon into bed, the same glorious Presence of the Holy Spirit pervaded and filled my being for hours, manifesting Himself in different ways in my body as I worshiped and praised the Lord, full of His love and joy and faith and peace and assurance. What a wonderful night of answered prayer in my life.

What really happened?

When I'm asked, "What all happened in your room that night?" I usually say the reason I don't tell all of that is that you might do what I did. You might get your eyes on manifestations and seek an experience like that. It would hinder you.

The point is: When did God fill me with the Spirit? Was it when I knew His glory and had those manifestations that night? No! It was in that prayer room I actively *received* (took) the Holy Spirit (His Person in person) and knew it was settled, feelings or no feelings!

Then He manifested Himself in different ways and also with different gifts "*as He wills*," as Paul clearly teaches in First Corinthians 12.

Now I should tell you about new developments as God began to work in new (to me) and wonderful ways in my life and ministry. I hesitate to speak about any specific gifts, but, for one thing, I began to have a new and very real faith in my life, trusting the Lord for everything, including my finances.

I began to know and experience a wonderful guidance in every way. And isn't that one of the real results? Was it not so even with Jesus? And doesn't Paul say that "*as many as are led by the Spirit of God, these are sons of God*?" (Romans 8:14, emphasis added).

Full control and complete guidance: These are major marks of the Spirit-filled life.

There is no room here to tell of my growing ministries and revivals also in Norway, where the Lord led me when I didn't know anyone there except one man. I met and married my wife there. And all the ministries of the "Revival Prayer Fellowship" and "Ministers' Prayer Fellowship" along with all the other unfoldings of the Lord followed in my life.

It has, by His grace, been a wonderful life:

.

and my wife (who speaks English now) says: "It's getting gooder and gooder."

She, by the way, has a precious testimony on how the Lord met her and also filled her with the Holy Spirit. She is my "better half" and I want you to read the testimony I asked her to write so I could include it in this book.

But, before I leave you, let me ask: *Have you been filled with the Holy Spirit? Are you sure?*

Why don't you pause to pray right now:

> Dear Lord, make this very clear to me by Your Word and by Your Holy Spirit. If there is any doubt about it in my heart and mind as to whether I have definitely and personally received the Holy Spirit, I receive Him *now*! And with all my heart I thank You, and trust Him to manifest Himself in my life "as He wills."

He is more willing to give than we are to receive. He says so: "If you then, being evil, know how to give good gifts to your children, *how much more* will your heavenly Father *give the Holy Spirit to those who ask Him!*" (Luke 11:13, emphasis added).

To God be the glory!

I should have made this number one, because it is number one.

Prayer got me into the Spirit-filled life, and the Spirit-filled life got me into prayer in a new and much enlarged way.

I early saw prayer as the greatest secret in the Christian life and ministry. I saw that if I am to learn the way of revival I must learn to pray and somehow develop a strong prayer life. Nothing is more important.

Now the Holy Spirit enlarged it and also made the Bible come alive as never before, making it my supreme prayer book.

Prayer has for me become ministry—my number one ministry and the ministry out of which all other ministry comes alive and becomes God's ministry.

Instead of just praying about things, I'm learning to bring things about by prayer.

Prayer is not everything, but I'm learning to do everything by prayer.

I don't want anything in my life that is not related to prayer. And if God wants me to pray about everything, it means He wants to answer about everything.

I want my whole life and ministry to be a

continual answer to prayer. If God means to do all He has promised to do in answer to prayer (and He does), then my greatest prayer is "Lord, teach me to pray."

8

Reidun's Testimony

Reidun, my wife, was filled with the Holy Spirit not long after we were married. She had been converted to Christ in Oslo, Norway where she was studying to become a nurse. She is a native of Tromsoe, Norway. Oslo then was in the grip of one of the great spiritual awakenings of our time. I'll let her tell her own story:

My life was changed when I received Jesus into my heart as my Savior. I wanted to be like Him; my desires had changed. I longed to please Him.

As I studied His Word and became acquainted with His ways, a deeper longing for the Holy Spirit to be a reality in my life was growing. Daily I would take time to read His Word and pray, and I began to pray that I might be filled with the Holy Spirit. This went on for some months, and the Lord showed me my own lack of full consecration.

When Jesus reached me that night in Oslo and became my Savior, I thought nothing would ever take His peace away from me. However, when I prayed now, He showed me that I was not full of the Holy Spirit, but so often wanted my own way. I often wept as I prayed as He revealed things in my life that grieved Him. I longed to be a vessel for His use. Then He convicted me of past sins which I had never confessed and needed to face and repent of.

The Importance of Honesty

One, for example, had to do with honesty. Years ago, as a girl, I had stolen some money and never confessed it to my school teacher who was involved in it. What made it doubly hard for me to confess was that she was not a Christian. I tried to "forget" it, but the Lord let me have no peace. I could not wiggle out of it!

So I committed it all to Him, asked His forgiveness at the same time that I wrote to this teacher. In my letter I asked for her forgiveness and also sent money "with interest," making restitution.

A remarkable thing happened. This teacher never answered me—for six years. And then I got news that she had died. But on her deathbed a minister led her to faith in Christ. She was not able to speak, but the Lord reminded her of my letter; so she wrote a note to me that all was forgiven and we would meet in heaven someday.

What a lesson! I learned how living faith came along the line of my obedience. Faith and obedience—what a wonderful pair!

So one night I drove down a stake and told the Lord I believed Him right then to fill me with His Spirit. *And He did*!

I started a new chapter and began to learn new precious lessons in prayer and intercession and a deeper and closer walk with the Lord. I am still learning. I saw Jesus in a new way, so precious and wonderful! The Holy Spirit came and glorified Jesus and continues to do so after these many years.

9

Marie Monsen's Testimony

Who was Marie Monsen? I heard about her in my different trips and ministries in Norway. Norway sent out many strong missionaries, and Marie Monsen was one of the strongest. She was a Lutheran lady who hungered for revival, prayed a lot for it and paid the full price to get it. She reminded me of Dr. Jonathan Goforth's experiences in his revivals in China. When she came into the experience and knew she was filled with the Spirit, things began to happen, and her meetings became very powerful. Even strong leaders like Dr. James ("Jim") Graham were revived in her meetings. When she preached "you must be born again," you knew what she meant, and you knew that you must be born again!

When I heard about her so much, then read

some of her writings and then read her story, I wanted you to know it. It is directly in line with what I have been teaching in this book and with what I have experienced.

Her fellow missionary tells the story:

Marie's Story

Marie Monsen, now in heaven, was a Norwegian Lutheran Missionary deep in a northern province of China. She arrived there in or about 1912. She was well trained for her task and was a born-again Christian. Fifteen years, including two furloughs, were spent in the ordinary work of a missionary. Increasingly, however, she felt the need of more power in her life and message. She longed to see the "greater things" spoken of in John 1:50 and 14:12. She longed for Acts 1:8 to be fulfilled in her life. It seems there was no one in the Mission who could assist her into a deeper knowledge and fellowship with the Lord Jesus.

In her desperation, *for six months* she sought to be filled with the Holy Spirit. One day at the end of this heart-searching and praying, with her open Bible, she heard a voice, the Lord's voice, saying, "Marie, this is received by faith."

Immediately she was cleansed and over-

172

whelmed with the love of God shed abroad in her heart by the Holy Spirit according to Romans 5:5. She knew it was "the baptism of the Holy Spirit." For it was after the Lord spoke faith to her that she at once fell to her knees and said, "Lord, I take it by faith."

Her soul was flooded with the joy of the Lord. This baptism was in 1927, shortly after another missionary promised the Lord that he would give much time to prayer and fasting for a mighty revival to sweep over China if he were healed of the terrible smallpox of which he was dying. He was healed instantly.

About the same time Dr. John Sung was filled with the Holy Spirit in New York City. He became the Charles Finney of China! For fifteen years he went up and down the length of China preaching the gospel. Multitudes turned to the Lord. Some of those converts became preachers of the gospel of Jesus Christ and saw many converted to Him.

Miss Monsen was released to go into evangelistic work. She used to say, "The only way you can get me for meetings is to pray me there." She also would say, "Do not pick unripe fruit; it will not keep."

Her work was thorough, bringing converts through to "the full assurance of faith."

10

Lewi Pethrus' Testimony

When I read the testimony and teaching of Lewi Pethrus, I felt I must include it in this book. It is full of good teaching and help. I found it in his book *The Wind Bloweth Where It Listeth*.

This book is very valuable, coming from Lewi Pethrus, the founder and leader of the Pentecostal movement in Sweden.

Years ago I first learned of this book through Dr. Harry Lindblom, pastor of an Evangelical Free Church in Chicago. He was a great preacher and knew the Holy Spirit as few did. He could preach fluently and fervently and also eloquently in both English and Swedish. He also had strong meetings in Sweden and was a close friend of Lewi Pethrus. He also translated Pethrus' book into English.

It will interest you to know (Harry Lindblom told me this story) that on one of his trips to the U.S., Pethrus was scheduled to speak in many Pentecostal churches. But he felt that there was too much that was loose and extreme where he had already gone and that he was not free to go on like this. So he asked Harry Lindblom, his good friend, to help him to reschedule some of the meetings. He did so and also helped Pethrus as one of his interpreters.

Lindblom had scheduled me for special revival meetings in his Chicago church, and during that time he told me this story.

Pethrus refers to the filling as the "baptism" of the Holy Spirit—quite a standard term then. The important thing is the way he teaches the "entering in" process. Here are some highlights:

> The first requisite for the baptism with the Holy Spirit is a clean heart and salvation from all known sin (see Acts 15:8-9). This should always be the starting point for any blessing God has promised to give. As soon as impurities arise in the heart, the conscience makes it known, and the Holy Spirit will not enter in fullness.

I have noticed very often that when individuals seek the baptism of the Spirit they begin to right the wrongs of the past. They get busy writing letters, going to others, asking forgiveness, making things right and correcting such things they thought would pass unnoticed. When all conscious sin has been taken away, then we really are in a place where it becomes easy to trust Him. He puts His seal upon a heart that is honest and clean.

The pathway to the baptism of the Holy Spirit leads also to the place of prayer (Luke 11:13, Acts 1:12-14). The individual who had been cleansed in the blood and to the best of his understanding and ability yields to God will live a life devoted to prayer. Prayer becomes the joy of life and the atmosphere and environment in which that soul lives and has its being. Time must be given to prayer, if this experience is to be realized.

There is one very important point concerning the reception of the baptism of the Holy Spirit, and that is that we comply with the words of the Lord and receive it "by faith." In Galatians 3:14 we read these words, "That the blessing of Abraham might come on the Gentiles through Jesus Christ; that we might receive the promise of the Spirit through faith." It is impossible to receive any spiritual blessing by any other means than faith.

Many have encountered difficulties at just this point. The way of faith had in many instances been mystified and distorted. There is not a truth or doctrine of Scripture that the unspiritual and disobedient do not warp and distort. Some say they have received the baptism of the Spirit by faith but have had no experience. This is a serious mistake. It would be like saying, "I am saved but have never experienced salvation." This is distorting the way of faith. The opposite is true. A real faith always brings a real experience.

But we must first believe before the experience comes. It is a grave mistake to wait until the experience comes before we dare to believe. Then we would believe our experience rather than God. I have noticed among certain groups that they are so concerned about the experience that they are actually hindered in their reception of the baptism.

My word to you, dear friends, seeking the baptism is "Dare to trust God." Satan will tempt you with the thought, *What if it does not hold?* Remember there is nothing so sure as the fact that God will keep His promise. We read the promise of the Spirit is received by faith. It is most important that we do not put our striving and agonizing in the place of faith. Faith is rest and trust.

We have a full right to lay our hands upon the promise of God and say, "Father, I am unworthy, but Jesus, Thy Son, has purchased me with His own precious blood. The baptism of the Spirit belongs to me. I lay my hand on Your Word and believe this is for me. Thank You, dear Father, I have that for which I prayed."

We see his stress on faith as *the* "way in." Then the feelings, the filling aspect, the experience, the manifestation(s) come "as He wills." Pethrus did go through many things and many testings, especially in regard to receiving by faith and not going by feelings. Later He was given the gift of tongues without seeking them.

Where he stresses receiving "the baptism" by faith, I have stressed the *Person* . . . and that we are to receive (take) *Him*. And then He does the manifesting "as He wills." This is the word and way of the Lord.

11

Billy Graham's Testimony

$\mathcal{I}$never knew Billy's full testimony concern-ing the Holy Spirit until recently, when I read it in Dr. Sherwood Wirt's book *Billy*.

I've known Billy for many years and have been with him a lot, at times also on his team in various crusades. In his New York crusade in 1957 I got to know Stephen Olford, who was also on the team there.

I did not know Stephen's story either—how God used him in 1946 to help Billy into the Spirit-filled life.

I've known Sherwood Wirt also, and we have been close friends for many years. When he was pastor of a Presbyterian church in the San Fran-cisco Bay area he used to come to our revival conferences for preachers and leaders, at Mt.

Hermon, California. Sherwood also came to our other church meetings as he was on the stretch for all that God had for him.

Sherwood just told me how he was in contact with Stephen Olford about Billy's precious experience of the Holy Spirit's infilling.

I should mention that I had known something concerning the Spirit in Billy's life. In the summer of 1949 we were both sitting together in the back row at a special Forest Home Conference where Dr. J. Edwin Orr was speaking on the Holy Spirit. No one was around where we sat, and all at once Billy turned to me and said he used to think we got it all when we are converted, but he did not think so now.

I never pursued this with Billy. But I do recall that after the great 1947 Los Angeles "breakthrough" Crusade, Billy would speak on the Holy Spirit's power and enduement, sometimes a night or two in his opening messages. But as so many were now praying for him all over the world, he no longer did that, but launched right into his evangelistic messages.

Now I got the full story from Sherwood Wirt. Here are the highlights:

In October 1946, when Billy was a

leading evangelist with Youth for Christ, he was scheduled to preach in Wales. There he heard Stephen Olford preach a strong message on the Scripture: "Be not drunk with wine, wherein is excess; but be filled with the Spirit." [Ephesians 5:18, KJV]

He lost no time getting to Stephen, and he told him he had preached on something he did not have and that he wanted the fullness of the Holy Spirit in his life too.

That led to them spending two days together about it in a hotel. The first day was spent in studying the Scriptures about it—searching in two ways: searching the Word and letting the Word search them.

Billy meant business. Whatever the cost in dedication and full surrender, he faced it. There was a lot of praying, and there were tears. Suddenly, in the afternoon of the second day, Billy cried, "I see it; that's what I want." They were on their knees together. Billy took hold in prayer like Jacob who told God he would not let go unless God would bless him.

Soon Billy began to pace back and forth in the room, saying, "I have it! I'm filled. I'm filled. This is the turning point of my life. This will revolutionize my ministry."

Billy was scheduled to preach in a Baptist church that night. He preached differently, greatly anointed; and the Welsh miners filled the aisles—yes, it seemed that almost the whole audience wanted to rush forward at the invitation.

Billy Graham's ministry took a leap forward! He had new liberty, new power, new authority, and his mighty ministry began to shape up.

Stephen told his father that something happened to Billy Graham, and that the world is going to hear from him. Billy, he said, is going to make his mark in history.

The rest *is* history!

The Holy Spirit who filled him is turning his story into *His* story.

From Billy *by Sherwood Wirt, copyright ©
1997, pp. 28-29. Used by permission of Good
News Publishers/Crossway Books, Wheaton,
Illinois 60187.*

Conclusion

$\mathcal{I}$sn't it wonderful to learn from the great apostle John that we receive eternal life when we receive the Person of Christ, and that we enter the abundant Spirit-filled life when we receive the Person of the Holy Spirit?

I pray this book will help you to become a Spirit-filled Christian; and if you are one, that it will confirm and deepen your life in the fullness of Christ and His Holy Spirit.

Publications by Armin Gesswein

How Can I Be Filled with the Holy Spirit?

How to Overcome Discouragement (booklet)

With One Accord in One Place